Rhymes and Reasons

Copyright © 1971 by Holt, Rinehart and Winston of Canada, Limited

All Rights Reserved   ISBN 0-03-923386-3

Cover Design: Barry Rubin

It is illegal to reproduce any portion of this book except by special arrangement with the publishers. Reproduction of this material without authorization by any duplication process whatsoever is a violation of copyright.

Distributed in the United States of America by
Mine Publications, Inc.,
25 Groveland Terrace,
Minneapolis, Minnesota 55403

Published simultaneously in Great Britain by
Blond Educational, Ltd.,
Iliffe House, Oadby, Leicestershire, England.

Printed in Canada

1 2 3 4 5   75 74 73 72 71

Rhymes and Reasons

Nine Canadian Poets Discuss Their Work

John Robert Colombo

Managing Editor
The Tamarack Review

With questions by Roy Bentley

Holt, Rinehart and Winston of Canada, Limited
Toronto   Montreal

Aspects of English

General Editor:
Roy Bentley
*University of British Columbia
Former co-ordinator of English
Etobicoke Board of Education,
Metropolitan Toronto*

Other Titles in the Series

Five Modern Canadian Poets	Eli Mandel *York University*
The Canadian Short Story	Tony Kilgallin *University of British Columbia*
Contemporary Satire	David J. Dooley *St. Michael's College University of Toronto*
New Direction in Canadian Poetry	John Robert Colombo *Managing Editor Tamarack Review*
Art, Communication and Pop Kulch	Donald F. Theall *Chairman, Department of English McGill University*
The Writing and Reading of Poetry	Earle Birney *Former professor at University of British Columbia and award-winning poet*
Eight Modern Canadian Poets	Eli Mandel *York University*
Film Appreciation	Gerald Pratley *Director, Ontario Film Theatre at Ontario Science Centre, C.B.C. Film Critic*

ACKNOWLEDGEMENTS

GEORGE BOWERING: To the author for "Locus Solus" from *Points on the Grid*; "Moon Shadow" from *The Man in Yellow Boots*; "Inside the Tulip" from *The Silver Wire;* "The Egg" from *The Gangs of Kosmos;* "Early Afternoon in the Rainy Season" from *Sitting in Mexico*. "The Grass" from *Rocky Mountain Foot* by George Bowering, reprinted by permission of The Canadian Publishers, McClelland and Stewart Limited, Toronto.

DAVID HELWIG: To the author for "Elegy," "Balearic Winter," "Poem for the End of the Revolution." "Sunday," "Grass Seed," "A Shaker Chair" are reprinted from *The Sign of the Gunman* by David Helwig by permission of Oberon Press.

GEORGE JONAS: To the author for "Broad Street, New York," "Hotel Royal, Budapest," "Emile X, Student Revolutionary," "On a State Funeral," "The Circle Narrows" from *The Happy Hungry Man;* "Five Stanzas on Perfection" from *The Absolute Smile*.

LIONEL KEARNS: To the author for "Bleeding Poem," "Foreign Aid," "Telephone" from *By the Light of the Silvery McLune: Media Parables, Poems, Signs, Gestures and Other Assaults on the Interface* by Daylight Press, Vancouver. "Presence," "It," "Friday at the Ex" from *Pointing* by Lionel Kearns by permission of The Ryerson Press, McGraw-Hill.

GWENDOLYN MacEWEN: To the author for "When I Think About it," "Meditations of a Seamstress (1)," "Meditations of a Seamstress (2)," "Written after Coming Out of a Deep Sleep." "You Held Out the Light" from *The Shadow Maker* by Gwendolyn MacEwen by permission of The Macmillan Company of Canada Limited. "Manzini: Escape Artist" from *Breakfast for Barbarians* by Gwendolyn MacEwen by permission of The Ryerson Press, McGraw-Hill.

TOM MARSHALL: To the author for "Song" and "West Street." "Autobiographies," "Words in Exile," "Interior Monologue #666," "Riding in Colin's Boat" from *The Silence of Fire* by Tom Marshall by permission of The Macmillan Company of Canada Limited.

JOHN NEWLOVE: To the author for "By the Church Wall" from *Moving in Alone*, © 1965 by John Newlove, Contact Press, Toronto; "She," "Dream," "Elephants" from *Elephants, Mothers & Others*, © 1963 by John Newlove, Periwinkle Press, Vancouver. "The Engine and the Sea" from *The Cave* and "Ride Off Any Horizon" from *Black Night Window* by John Newlove, reprinted by permission of the Canadian Publishers, McClelland and Stewart Limited, Toronto.

ALDEN NOWLAN: To the author for "The Bull Moose," "The Execution," "Walking toward the Bus Station." "I, Icarus" from *Bread, Wine and Salt* by Alden Nowlan, © 1967 by Clarke, Irwin and Company Limited. Used by permission. "Alpha and Omega" and "On the Nature of Human Compassion" from *The Mysterious Naked Man* by Alden Nowlan, © 1969 by Clarke, Irwin and Company Limited. Used by permission.

J. MICHAEL YATES: To the author for "In Memoriam: Peter Paul Fersch," "Canticle for Electronic Music #4." "Again and again I go away" and "I persist in a little fabric" from *The Great Bear Lake Meditations* by J. Michael Yates by permission of Oberon Press. "Maria" and "In the blood-coloured cage" from *Hunt in an Unmapped Interior* by J. Michael Yates, by permission of The Golden Quill Press.

Care has been exercised to trace ownership of copyright material contained in this text. The publishers will gladly receive information that will enable them to rectify any reference or credit in subsequent editions.

CONTENTS

PREFACE 1
Reading the Poem

GEORGE BOWERING 10

Locus Solus 11
Moon Shadow 13
Inside the Tulip 15
The Grass 16
The Egg 17
Early Afternoon in the Rainy Season 18

DAVID HELWIG   20

    Sunday   21
    Grass Seed   22
    A Shaker Chair   23
    Elegy   27
    Balearic Winter   29
    Poem for the End of the Revolution   31

GEORGE JONAS   35

    Broad Street, New York   36
    Hotel Royal, Budapest   37
    Emile X, Student Revolutionary   39
    On a State Funeral   41
    The Circle Narrows   43
    Five Stanzas on Perfection   44

LIONEL KEARNS   46

    Presence   47
    It   48
    Friday at the Ex   49
    Bleeding Poem   52
    Foreign Aid   58
    Telephone   59

GWENDOLYN MACEWEN 65

You Held Out the Light 66
Manzini: Escape Artist 66
When I Think About It 68
Meditations of a Seamstress (1) 69
Meditations of a Seamstress (2) 70
Written after Coming out of a Deep Sleep 71

TOM MARSHALL 73

Autobiographies 74
Words In Exile 75
Interior Monologue #666 78
Riding in Colin's Boat 79
Song 81
West Street 82

JOHN NEWLOVE 84

By the Church Wall 85
She 87
The Engine and the Sea 88
Ride Off any Horizon 90
Dream 95
Elephants 96

ALDEN NOWLAN 97

The Execution 98
The Bull Moose 99
On the Nature of Human Compassion 101
Alpha and Omega 101
I, Icarus 103
Walking toward the Bus Station 104

J. MICHAEL YATES 106

In Memoriam: Peter Paul Fersch 108
Maria 112
"Again and again I go away" 113
"I persist in a little fabric" 114
"In the blood-coloured cage" 115
Canticle for Electronic Music #4 115

OTHER PUBLICATIONS 117

Preface

I selected the poets in this anthology but the poets selected the poems. I invited nine Canadian poets to make selections from their published and unpublished poetry that could represent the total body of their work to date. Although the choice of individual poems was left to the poet, the number of selections was limited to six for each writer, and I did request poems that would be reasonably accessible to the reader on first reading. I concluded my invitation with a further request: Would each poet kindly include a prose commentary to accompany his or her poetry? *Rhymes and Reasons* is the result.

And what about the result? The poets have made this a collection of brand-new poetry. Hardly any of the poems in *Rhymes and Reasons* have appeared in any other poetry anthology or textbook (although the poets themselves are well represented in both). Almost half of these poems have never before appeared between the covers of books; almost a quarter have never been published before at all. This is an "active anthology" of new poetry.

The commentaries are equally new and on-going. Some are literary creations in their own right: prose poems, personal essays, snatches of autobiography. Others are not unlike literary guidebooks: full of directions, explanations, suggestions for things to see. All the commentaries give clues to the current preoccupations of the poets concerned, and each commentary might be viewed as offering some valuable but incidental information. The poetry can be appreciated without reading the commentaries, but the commentaries add something to the poems. What they add is the human element. Were these nine poets to appear one beside the other on a platform to recite their poems, rather than one after the other in the pages of a book, they would bring to their readings subtleties of accent and expression, varieties of meaning and mood. And they would probably preface their poems with comments like those found in these prefaces. The commentaries are no substitute for the poets-in-the-flesh but they do aid in establishing the personalities of the poets and the contexts within which to respond to their poems.

What do these nine poets have in common? Certainly not subjects or styles or themes; rather social realities. Born in the thirties, they grew up in the forties and came intellectually and legally of age in the fifties. This is the same decade Maxwell Geismar has dubbed "The Fatal Fifties" for the tone of these ten years was set by the Cold War waged by the U.S.S.R. and the U.S.A. and the gradual Americanization of Canada. This was not an easy period in which to be a poet, especially in the northern part of the North American continent. Although all nine poets are now Canadian citizens, one left Hungary for Toronto, and another the United States for Vancouver.

The decade that saw the emergence of the Beat poets was followed by "The Psychedelic Sixties" which saw the emergence of the Hippies. Suddenly the Cold War was thawing, Canadians were becoming aware of their national identity, and things were better for all the arts. From one corner of Canada to the other, little magazines began to make their appearance. These were mimeograph or offset publications of no particular beauty, but they were filled with exciting poems and new bylines. They bore such titles as *Tish, Moment, Evidence, Open Letter*. Just as Marshall McLuhan formulated his thoughts in the pages of a little magazine called *Explorations,* so a whole host of new poets came into their own in the pages of dozens of ephemeral but highly serious publications. Two well-known poets who arrived by taking the little-magazine route were Alfred Purdy and Milton Acorn—as well as many included in this anthology. Were these young poets reading any older Canadian writers? They read everything they could lay their hands on by Raymond Souster, Irving Layton, Louis Dudek, but they also read seriously the work of dozens of contemporary American poets.

During the Sixties the decisive influence on Canadian poetry was American poetry. In a way this was unfortunate because

American poetry was divided into two large opposing groups—those using traditional forms vs. those using avant-garde forms, the academic poets vs. the beat poets. By the end of the Sixties a truce was called in this aesthetic Civil War and most of the fighting died down, but some skirmishes were still being waged north of the 49th by Canadian participants. In other ways the American influence was a healthy one because such writers as William Carlos Williams and Robert Lowell, Allen Ginsberg and Richard Wilbur, were, above all else, whatever their allegiances, regardless of the labels others pinned on them, excellent poets well worth reading and learning from.

Canada is a more tolerant—or patient—country than the United States. Instead of grouping poets into "either/or" categories, here writers could range themselves into a spectrum. In Western Canada there was the *Tish* group, centred around a magazine of that name published by young lecturers at the University of British Columbia who wrote in the "Black Mountain style"—a kind of dramatic utterance. In Central Canada there was the "mythopoeic school," which was not really a school, but a few Ontario poets who wrote formally but with a flavour of myth and archetype. Some had studied literary symbolism under Northrop Frye of the University of Toronto, and one of them published a magazine called *Alphabet*. In Eastern Canada there were those Maritime writers who were loosely associated with *The Fiddlehead,* a quarterly published by the University of New Brunswick in Fredericton. The Maritimes themselves played a large role in poems by these poets, both as subject and as setting.

Rhymes and Reasons represents the work of all three groups. George Bowering and Lionel Kearns emerged from the pages of *Tish*. The "mythopoeic school" influenced the oracular poems of Gwendolyn MacEwen. The leading writer of the Maritime group is Alden Nowlan. But there are other poets who remain unaffiliated in *Rhymes and Reasons* because a Canadian writer does not have to relate to any group or region of the country in order to be taken seriously as a poet. David Helwig and Tom Marshall edit *Quarry* in Kingston, Ontario, but *Quarry* has no group identity. John Newlove and J. Michael Yates have both lived in Vancouver, but neither was a member of the *Tish* group. George Jonas writes in

Toronto, but he does not belong to any group, school or coterie. Poets are, above all, individuals. And Canada is a country that by its very constitution encourages variety and individuality.

But while these poets were writing, Canadian literature was expanding, and changing. The most discerning editor this country has ever known was busy all through the Fifties reading more than a hundred and fifty years of Canadian and pre-Canadian poetry and verse. His aim was to compile *The Oxford Book of Canadian Verse,* which was published in the first year of the new decade. In the introduction, A. J. M. Smith discussed the characteristics of Canadian poetry both past and present.

> The Canadian poet has one advantage—an advantage that derives from his position of separateness and semi-isolation. He can draw upon French, British, and American sources in language and literary convention; at the same time, he enjoys a measure of detachment that enables him to select and adapt what is relevant and useful. This gives to contemporary Canadian poetry in either language a distinctive quality—its eclectic detachment. This can be, and has been, a defect of timidity and mediocrity; but it can also be, as it is hoped this book will show, a virtue of intelligence and discrimination.

The Canadian poet, according to Smith, is "detached" or aloof from world history, an observer rather than a participant. His work is "eclectic," for he has consciously followed poetic models from here and there in time and space. Above all, the Canadian poet has "intelligence" and "discrimination" (not their contraries, passion and involvement).

Smith's judgment was, perhaps, truer of the past than it would be of the future. Early in the Sixties, when so many new poets began to appear in print, his publishers asked him to revise and enlarge *The Oxford Book of Canadian Verse,* which by now was the standard anthology in the field. Smith set to work only to discover that what he really needed was not a new edition but a new book—a totally new book, one that would concentrate on living poets. *Modern Canadian Verse* was published in the Centennial Year. After reading so much contemporary poetry, Smith saw things differently:

> Instantaneous communication, electronic and nuclear devices, and the universal half-education supplied by the mass-media have created a

very self-conscious world divided into economic and ideological clusters but united by a common fear of possible annihilation. As a result, Canadian poetry in the fifties and sixties has become more like modern poetry in the United States, England, and France, and less like Canadian poetry in the nineteenth century. . . . Local, regional, and national influences, whether geographic or social, are ceasing to be of first importance. If no man is an island, neither is any nation an island, even so huge and mainly an empty one as Canada.

Now the Canadian poet, according to Smith, lives in a country like other countries ("economic and ideological clusters") and shares problems and possibilities with poets in these other countries. There are common poetic influences from New York, London and Paris. Poets are no longer eclectic and detached in Canada.

But are they passionate and involved? That is for the reader to decide.

Reading the Poems

A poem reverberates; it creates a series of echoes within the reader so that, as Alden Nowlan says, the reader shares in the creation of the poem. This, of course, does not always happen. Sometimes the inexperienced reader cannot find a way *into* a poem; he may read around it or about it—but he is not reading the poem. In this book, the poets' comments may help the reader to a deeper understanding of the poems; the comments may tell you more about the poet or about the incident which inspired the poet than about the actual poem. But it is the poem with which the reader is concerned; the poem itself is what should be read and re-read until it has a chance to reverberate. Occasionally, the reader will still have difficulty and so to help him questions have been included. The questions are not designed to worry the poem to death, but to help to "open" one pathway to its understanding. Use the questions if you find them helpful—better still, ask your own questions, more effective ones, different ones, additional ones. Or make a poem of your own on a theme similar to the theme of the poem you are reading, and compare the two. This is probably the best way to understand and enjoy poetry.

R. B.

The Poets

George Bowering

"He is a gifted poet—with the gift of energy," Phyllis Webb wrote about George Bowering. Born in the Okanagan Valley in 1935, the poet and writer was educated at the University of British Columbia where he was a prominent member of the Tish group in the early 1960's. His recent books include Mirror on the Floor *(a novel)*, Alfred Purdy *(a critical monography)*, and Rocky Mountain Foot *and* The Gangs of Kosmos *(books of poetry for which the author received the Governor General's Award in 1970)*. George Bowering teaches in the English Department of Sir George Williams University, Montreal.

I might be considered a romantic poet in that I believe nature to be the best instructor. Romantic poets tend to join primitives, children, & crazy people in believing that the natural environment is trying to tell them something. Instead of praying or preaching I now write poems. I think that the poetic act is largely in realizing the common energy that runs through the nature in me & the nature I find myself among. A great number of my poems deal with that realization, & most of them are informed by it. I think that poems, souls, governments, & families begin to fail when there is something thrust between them & the details of the natural world. A good (bad) example would be billboards. Another would be garbage on the water. Another would be authoritarian censorship. For examples of other poems that treat the subject well, I would direct you to Shelley's "Ode to the West Wind," Olson's "Songs of Maximus," & Birney's "Billboards Build Freedom of Choice." The desire to affirm a love for nature leads me to write of the forest & the river, of course, but it also leads me to seek ways to compose my poems according to what I can learn of my own natural composition. Knowing that the opposers of nature always place themselves above her ways, I am determined to place my self, according to my nature, beside nature, to imitate nature, as William Carlos Williams said. So I examine the workings of my body's faculties as would a naturalist in examining the features of a seashore, for instance. The poems work, therefore, when the actor called the mind is not ruler of the others (breath, hearing, balance, *etc.*), but a participant with them in the acts of perception & the recording of those acts. I would hope above all that the readers try to respond in a similar way, with democratic bodies.

The six poems I have chosen are taken from six of my books, & show part of my response to six traditional features of nature as seen in much poetry: mountain, moon, flower, grass, egg, & a man found in the midst of the big city in which nature is to be found everywhere to an extent not to be believed by people who live in the cities of North America.

LOCUS SOLUS

Attaching toes to Vancouver downtown sidewalks over-
sluiced with rain water

               under billowed concave black
umbrella dripping around me

               eye down on neon reflections
wiggled in the gutter
           cursing & moving alone
next to shoulders of down looking strangers
soggy in the rain

I remember dried out lips & tongue
                  long trip without water-
bottle down the side of old Blue Mountain

It was a hundred & twenty
                        in the shade
                        but there was no shade
& coming down was harder than going up
down in the empty water-
drainage slashes
                        in dust now
                        & over boulder slides

Finally down
to lichen green rocks
                        & face first into the stream muddied
                        by the dog a few yards up
head pusht into the water
teeth aching & belly pulled tight by the cold sucking
                                        down the throat

& the final walking home
                        respecting the sun & taking it easy
                        planting feet in long easy strides

For Bowering, a significant word in the poem is "down." Why might "water" be a more significant word? Can you suggest other titles for the poem?

I come from the South Okanagan, where the main features of nature are sun (because it is very bright & hot) & water (because it is scarce, & you must think about it in all your plans). When I moved to Vancouver I got more water than I ever wanted falling on my head. The way I hear the poem, nine years after I wrote it, the change rings on the word "down." I look at the people forced to look down in the first part of the poem, & see the two boys & the dog working their way down to water so that the water may work its way down inside them. In the city the people protect themselves from water, the source of life. At the foot of the mountain water means your lips will turn from white to their natural color, & you do not see anything wrong with sharing it with your dog. You are not his "master." Neither is the mountain yours.

MOON SHADOW

Last night the rainbow
round the moon

climbed with how sad steps
as I walkt home

color surrounding me
cloud around my head.

      I am moon!
      Arrows fly at me!!

      I slide cold & pale
      over cold earth
      of Alberta winter!

      I show one face
      to the world,
      immaculate still,
      inscrutable female
      male animal ball
      of rock
      shining with borrowed light

      rolling in that light
      the other side of
      forgetful space!

I am a shining tear
of the sun

full moon, silver,

George Bowering

who but myself knows
where the sun shall set?

I am able to instruct
the whole universe,
instruct the heart,
the weeping eye
of any single man.

Slide over the moon-
lit earth, a shadow
of a chariot.

      Walk homeward
forgetful where I have been

with how sad steps
my shadow before me

on the earth, moon shadow
rainbow round my heart,
wondering where in the universe I am.

Should stanzas 8, 9, 10 and 11 be indented to correspond with stanzas 4, 5, 6 and 7?

Traditionally the moon makes lunatics of men so that they may instruct their people who have separated the parts of life too far from one another. The poem seems intent on joining parts that rime with one another, giving testimony against their unreal divorces. Maybe that's why the moon has so wan a face. The weeping eye has the shape of the moon, of the rainbow, of the sun, the tear, the universe itself. The light on the earth at night is given by the moon, & it bounced there from the sun. No one owns it, certainly not the man, whose eye it is reflected in. The person in the poem becomes lost, as one becomes lost in the forest, not as one is lost in his role. Like the light, he is part male, part female, part mineral, part water. He is walking with sad steps but there is a rainbow. He contains & reflects contraries, but he is not uneasy about this.

INSIDE THE TULIP

Inside the tulip
we make love
on closer look
seeing faint green lines, new

let me share this flower
with you, kiss you
press my tongue on pollen
against the roof of my mouth

Look at me long enough
& I will be a flower
or wet blackberries dangling
from a dripping bush

Let me share you
with this flower, look
at anything long enough
& it is water

on a leaf, on a petal
where we lie, bare legs together

What is the significance of the words "..........look / at anything long enough / & it is water"?

George Bowering 15

It is a love poem, & the lady is loved in the way all nature's beauty is loved, not so much because the love has been earned, but because it just happens. The poem's suggestion may be that love is not blind but rather more acutely sighted. It may collapse the necessity of contiguous logic to showing that people are part of the garden. I don't think God made the garden to be owned or managed by Adam & Eve. I think they were part of its moving beauty. If I were to say that I can see roses in your cheeks, I would mean it literally. Poets are literalists of the imagination. After dinner you might even have wet blackberries in your stomach. The poet Gary Snyder said that he wants to be left out in the bush when he dies, so that animals can eat him.

THE GRASS

I must tell you
of the brown grass
that has twenty times
this year appeared
from under the
melting snow, reared
its version of spring
like a sea-lion coming
out of water, a-dazzle
in the sun, this
brave grass the sun
will only burn again
returning like a tiny
season.

What words used earlier in the poem give meaning to the last two lines?

This little poem has one mistake in it—a simile, but it is not as bad as it could be, because the simile is at least also taken from nature, to show the concert of bravery & beauty in the animal world & the vegetable world; & naturally my admiration & impulse ("I must tell you") also connect the human world. The simile supports the better metaphor made by the rime of the stressed "season" & "sea-lion" & "sun"—they combine to make bravery & beauty in a season when people cut off from roots tend to be most depressed.

THE EGG

The egg sat on the workbench
for weeks, me passing it every day
in my search for tools, cobwebs,
five years old, looking for

the machines of life. The source
of life, I knew, as mysterious as
my mother's bedroom. I didn't touch
the egg for weeks, my brain resembling

its contours. Till the day came
I gave up waiting for the news, I
contrived to make it roll & fall
to the floor beside a rusted shovel.

Bending over, I knew first the
terrible stink, & then the quills
of light, bone, or fiber, it was
a wing never to be used. It's guilt

I carried for a year & then carried
lighter for more years, as if I
myself smelled, as if I had brought
those tender stinking wings to earth.

George Bowering

This poem is packed with rime because nature teaches us rime, & this poem is from a series of poems about learning from nature in childhood. It is no accident that the egg is like a head, & I am an egghead. It was no accident, either, that the egg fell, but why was it on the bench. As a poet, now I am doing what I was doing then, at five, looking for tools, the machines of life. The poem is a machine made of words, & the brain, eye, body, are all soft machines. The universe is, as far as we can imagine, the largest machine of all, but as Sir James Jeans said, it begins to look more like a giant thought. But why guilt? For some years after that I took care of the chickens & could never eat them. I didn't know then that they would likely eat me if they could, without thinking too much about it.

EARLY AFTERNOON IN THE RAINY SEASON

Days like this
words are
lockt
inside somewhere

Across the street here
an old man in loose blue coveralls
sits under a dancing cactus
cutting weeds

The rain hasnt come
but heavy clouds fall
in the slopes of green hills

The loose trees
wave in the wind
& I

wave also, here on an ancient lake

south of the Tropic of Cancer
I wave

the flowers on the water
loose, caught & solidified
in the giant murals of the city
as I, before this Spanish typewriter
shaking my head to release words, flowers

the colors of Mexico,
pink cloth waving on a loose line
The old man is now
looking at the sky, his hand
touching his cactus

His words
hang in the air
before his face

Bowering mentions "the slight suspension at the end of the line." In what ways, in action and mood, might the entire poem be regarded as being concerned with suspension and suspense?

The Aztecs wrote & drew pictures of men with words, glyphs, in front of their mouths. We with our alphabet tend to abstract too much, locking the words inside our minds, just as we make our cities as colorless as we can, promoting their isolating functions, erecting tall gray buildings instead of the bright-colored ones you see all over Mexico City. This poem tries to give a sense of a city in which people can keep loose because they have so much of the countryside among their buildings. So the words are there, right in front of your face—cactus, rain, clouds, hills, trees, lake, flowers, sky, because they are all around you in the city of seven million people who are also still related to their ancestors.

   I would like you to read this poem aloud (allowed), & recognize the slight suspension at the end of the line, & I'd like you to do that with all the poems. That is the sound approach.

George Bowering   19

David Helwig

"One of the most exciting poets to come along in a long time," Eli Mandel said about David Helwig. The poet and writer was born in Toronto in 1938 and educated at the University of Toronto, where he won many literary prizes, and the University of Liverpool. Figures in a Landscape and The Sign of the Gunman are two collections of his verse. He is also the author of a book of stories called The Streets of Summer. With Tom Marshall he has edited 14 Stories High. David Helwig teaches in the English Department of Queen's University, Kingston.

For me, poems are made out of the thoughts and feelings of everyday life. If I stand still for a moment, the reality of the sights and sounds that are near me begins to create some kind of pressure. I want to record what I perceive and feel, to work out what it all means. Love, politics, the beauty of things seen, my children and the feelings they create in me, any or all of these may begin to rattle my brain. I start to search for words, phrases to catch the truth of the moment. Sometimes the search ends abortively, but sometimes it goes on until I have a poem.

SUNDAY

Yesterday I saw two pigeons
coupling on a church spire,
the male with his wings up,
for one moment
arched and poised in space.

Today I see pigeons riding the wind,
sliding on its long open curves
as Maggie and I run through the park,
our hair chaotic in the wind,
our hair flying out from our heads
while Maggie tosses
a handful of dust into the air
to see it scatter and fly.

The wind is everywhere.
There is no Sunday stillness.
At the church across the park
the organ is playing,
but the wind breaks the song
into fragments blown about my ears.

Organ notes, dust,
hurtling pigeons,
my running daughter
are fragments
blown onto my eyes and ears.

And of such whirling fragments
we must make all love,
arched and poised,
short as the union of those pigeons.

Helwig searches for words "to catch the truth of the moment". In what ways are the words "arched and poised" the central words of the poem?

I'd been at a party the night before and had a hangover. I was perhaps more sensitive than usual to the sight of the bare ugly park where my daughter and I went to play. The details of the poem are all real. That's what I saw. I wanted to record it, and to record my feeling of how we grab a handful of meaning out of chaos.

GRASS SEED

The earth by our front door is
barren. What I plant dies, even
nasturtiums even marigolds that run
wild at the back of the yard.

Grass will grow anywhere. Dark on a
cold day, Kate comes and I come to plant
grass and Kate to throw seeds out to
the wind. The seeds of grass are light
and thrown, blow across autumn easily.

Her suit is pink like the insides of
things, of the mouth. She is pink
mischief among my planting, Kate and
the dark wind.

We are all light as blown seed. But
it grows anywhere. Young we are
soft as the insides of things. The
earth at our door is barren.

What is the difference in meaning between the first sentence and the last sentence of the poem?

Another poem built from a single real incident that only found its meaning in words when I found the image of the mouth which managed to make real for me the softness that we set against a hard world.

A SHAKER CHAIR

1

standing and moving
a rocking chair
slat and finial
of native wood
maple or hickory

plain as plain speaking
plain as hands
plain as silence
standing or moving

an angel hanging
above the lathe
standing and moving
with his white wing
ruled the pattern
cut by the hands

now in the chair
order and use
standing and moving

2

Out of the mills of Manchester came Ann Lee,
one of the hundred prophets those dark mills bred.
Hysterical with the loss of her four children,
she swore her blacksmith husband, Abraham,
would never lift his black body on her again,
then starved herself until her senses broke
and light poured through her like a waterfall.
They jailed her once for crying out in church
that they were evil in condoning marriage,
but prison only dignified her light.
There she exchanged the blacksmith's love for Christ's,
came out a martyr, God's new prophetess,
"Mother," she called herself, "of the new creation."
On the voyage to plant the word in the wilderness,
the ship was foundering till she prophesied
and all aboard were saved.
                              After her death
one Joseph Meacham became her vision's heir
and gave her wandering light order and form,
gave the converts a covenant.
                          These things:
They freely gave themselves and all their goods
for mutual support and benefit.
Debtors to God, they worked to improve their time,
celibate, industrious, reborn.
All members had a just and equal right
to the use of things according to their needs.

This, they said, was the resurrection life.

3

I see in the Shaker rocking chair
stillness turning, stillness moving,

contemplation and silent standing,
even the denial of the body.

Why should I blind this fire-nerved body
as you sit near in a favourite chair,
not love the passion of your moving
around me, love your walking, standing?

I think of a city with no house standing,
the photograph of a child's starved body,
silence set in the father's chair,
refugees on the road moving.

The resurrection life is a moving
in angel's stillness, a way of standing
apart, denying the loving body,
refusing to own so much as a chair.

4

I am not still, but blown about
by any gust of wind,
a scrap of sense, a leaf, cannot
take root, cannot grow
like a great maple tree, give shade,
ask for nothing but sun.

Only the green world eats the sun.
the rest must live on flesh.

My greedy hands care for the touch
of body, clutch of soul,
still grasping when they give the gifts
of gentleness, of care,
still counting coins of sense and kindness,
hands touch to hold.

David Helwig

5

To turn away to the light of God's solitude,
to deny the earth in denying ownership
is not for me. I must live in bone and flesh.

The Shakers had visions and dances for relief
for the discharge of the electricity of sense,
the need to grasp and hold. For dancing bones,
dancing in rings or dancing in the chains
of nerve and muscle still are dancing bones.

Near me tonight you read, curled in your chair,
and every lying light of your dying flesh
says Lebanon is laid between your breasts,
is not to be built in the cold stone of the world.

But as a man who thinks that we will be
just what we say we are, I find their speech,
the speech of men who sought a new Lebanon
in their common good, who burned with the solid flame
of heaven brought to earth, the speech of such,
Mennonite, Quaker, Shaker or Doukhobor,
haunts my hands as I reach toward your face.

And yet in spite of the silence of the chair,
I turn and move away from them to you,
my now and never, one unperfect love.

What questions are raised for the poet by the Shakers' beliefs? What are his answers?
What is the significance of the image of the Shaker chair in the first section of the poem?
What is the significance of the allusion in the second line of the second section?

I worked on this poem for a long time, mostly for several days when I was supervising the writing of examinations. Whenever I could, I'd sit at the desk in front of the room and work at pieces of the poem. Sometimes, even as I was walking among the desks, I'd work out lines. The poem contains a theme that is very important to me, the problem of possession, of owning, both in social terms and in terms of love. The pure communism of the Shakers fascinates me. Yet their solution to the stress of human love, absolute celibacy, avoids another kind of ownership by gesture which is, for me, too extreme. But the questions raised by their beliefs were terribly important to me, and I had to write the poem to try to work them out.

ELEGY

. . . later I found out that Julio Zenon Acosta had died on the hilltop. That uneducated and illiterate guajiro who had understood the enormous tasks which the Revolution would face after its victory, and who was learning the alphabet to prepare himself for this, would never finish that task.
—Che Guevara

Julio Zenon Acosta, did the Cuban bugs
pick your bones on that jungle hilltop
where you died twelve years ago?
Did the green snakes coil in your ribs?

In the days before that day
you walked through the dangerous hills
carrying supplies and the weight
of your gigantic hopes, one by one
adding the letters of the alphabet
to your kit. Dying too soon
your death was a silence, a screaming
hole in the world on a Cuban hilltop.

Waiting on that hilltop
at forty-five years old,
a peasant who gave his love
to the words of strangers
was killed in a surprise attack.

A man had betrayed your comrades. They ran
into the green of the deeper forest,
left blankets, medical supplies
and left your body,
one letter in a nightmare language
written on a Cuban hill
where your hope of words ended.

Twelve years later, Julio Acosta,
I imagine your bleached bones
somewhere in Cuba and your body
part of the Cuban earth, and I bring
these letters of my foreign alphabet
to speak of your interrupted task
and your wordless death.

Alphabet, letters, words and language are important words in this poem. Why?

Like many people, I was fascinated by the figure of Che Guevara, and I wrote a poem (not a very good one) at the time of his death. But then I went on to read his book on the revolution in Cuba and found the quotation at the head of this poem. It seemed to me to embody the meaning of the Cuban Revolution, the cost, the desperate faith, the hope of simple people for a better life.

BALEARIC WINTER

                        All afternoon, the wind
has come from the sea to beat on the white walls
    of the island. The trunks of the Balearic pines
are bent from its force, and all day long
    I've thought of Chopin wintering on Majorca,
setting on paper the dainty marvels of his brain
    while the delicate webbed grip of his lungs
on the precious air grew slack and shallow,
    and he coughed, tried not to breathe, listened to rain.

    Outside this room, the wind is fast and loud
against the windows and against the door
    that leads to our balcony. I sink in a chair
to work in the half light and whistle between my teeth
    a Chopin nocturne.

                        In the mornings here
the young *emigrés* from Europe and America
    sit outside a bar in the main square
or walk through the narrow white streets of the old city
    past doorways that lead to dark small rooms and windows
where caged birds sing. A boy and girl will sit
    in shelter against a wall, eating an orange.

Beside the road, daisies with yellow centres
    and single scarlet poppies are growing wild
among the almond trees, and by a white house
    the orange trees are thick and bright with fruit.

    In the afternoon, children walk on the beach
to gather shells, the miraculous common harvest
    of the shore, cowries, starfish, and all
the delicate architecture that is made
    and dies in the body of the sea, that children,

David Helwig

    wise and willful, gather in the lust of beauty
        and carry away, carrying to closed rooms
the faint smell of the sea.

                        Beside this sea
    shut up on Majorca, Chopin coughed in the rain
of the Balearic winter, an *emigré* writing down
        melodic effete nocturnes and songs in praise
of Poland where he did not live. While Sand
        comforted him and smoked and brooded and worked.

    Late in the afternoon, the sun, bright as a poppy,
drops westward to the Atlantic, always westward,
        like the gold that tempted west the burning eyes
of the conquistadors. Falling always, the sun
        drops into the ocean, under the Atlantic
to the golden sensual underwater cities
        that hang on the branches of the sea like oranges.

As the white walls darken and the island loses its gold,
        the *emigrés* smoke drugs in tiny rooms.
I drink white wine and coffee, and I think
        of those dainty effeminate fingers playing nocturnes
through all the wind and rain and fear of death
        of that Majorcan winter.

In what ways do the stories about Chopin provide a "centre for all the images and a focus for the themes of life and death, beauty and strength"?

After spending several months in England, to arrive in the Mediterranean on the island of Ibiza was a wonderful relief. But the day we arrived was cold and windy. Still, the island was overwhelmingly beautiful, covered with flowers, the houses fitting perfectly into the landscape. I wanted to write about it, but at first I had nothing but impressions, which I might send home on a postcard. But when I remembered the stories of Chopin on the nearby island of Majorca (most of my information coming from vague memories of an old movie with Cornell Wilde and Merle Oberon) I found I had a centre for all the images and a focus for the themes of life and death, beauty and strength. It's one of my favourite poems because I was very happy when I wrote it.

POEM FOR THE END OF THE REVOLUTION

The revolution is over
and never began, though
Winstanley dug up the commons
and Nechayev (Agent 2771
of the World Revolutionary
Alliance—which didn't exist)
killed the informer Ivanov
in the name of a future
which would not come
for we never knew
what time was, at least
not well enough.

(Alone on a moving bus
riding to Montreal,
the city of soldiers,
riding through a landscape
of rocks, rivers and the warm
colours of a dying year,
I thought of the hands
that closed the throat
of Pierre Laporte
and in the name of freedom.)

Marx said: "Time is

a locked spiral, and freedom
is knowing you were never free."

(As the bus drove into Cornwall,
the houses were so heavy
with the dust of life
that it seemed to me
I'd lived in every one.

And I found myself
looking at the windows,
the bare trees, grey sky,
here at the edge
of a strange town, remembering
what it was like
to be the child
of ordinary people
on an ordinary afternoon.)

And Tolstoy laboured
for a revolution too pure
to be touched by the hands of men.
He said: "Time is not real,
only love, only the Kingdom of God
is real. And I am getting old
and they will not give me peace."

(As we sat and talked
high over Montreal,
a woman's voice
from fifteen floors below
screamed wildly, angrily,
but all we could hear
were the letters FLQ.

My friend said

that if he spoke French
he would join
Le Parti Québecois,
but as it was
he only wanted a divorce,
a difficult matter
since his lawyer
was now in jail.)

The revolution goes round
and round. A dance,
the double dance
of politicians and killers,
dancing our history
into melodrama.

(The next day I arrived
in Fredericton where
there was no one
I had ever loved.)
The question is, what
was the question we could
never quite remember?
It had something to do
with the past, the future;
we say history, we say
the revolution, we say
what is beyond our being
that will hold in itself
childhood and death, work
and what we've loved.

We, you, I, them,
is, will be, was.

The revolution never began
and is never over.

Like everyone else in Canada, I was fascinated by the FLQ kidnappings. I tried one poem about the death of Laporte, but got nowhere with it. It was a time when I was travelling a lot, heard of the Laporte kidnapping in Ottawa, of the War Measures Act in Toronto. It was also a time of personal emotional upheaval. One day I found myself on a bus from Kingston to Montreal reading George Woodcock's book, *Anarchism*, and struggling to make sense of all that had happened. I began to make notes, and the next day I wrote more, this time on a plane between Montreal and Fredericton. I began to see the central paradox of the need for men to live as political animals while knowing the imperfection of any political order. At least since the Middle Ages, men have struggled with this paradox. The struggle finally comes down to a series of painful choices facing the individual. My own journey, my own confusion, is at the centre of the poem for this reason.

George Jonas

"Tough, sardonic, resonantly humane" are the words of Hayden Carruth that best characterize the poetry of George Jonas. The "poet-playwright-producer" (as he calls himself) was born in Budapest in 1935 and educated at the Hungarian Liberal Arts Faculty where he studied theatre and film. He left Hungary in 1956 and settled in Toronto. He is the author of two books of poetry, The Absolute Smile and The Happy Hungry Man, and a contributor to many anthologies and magazines. He has written numerous radio plays and is the Chief Story Editor of the Canadian Broadcasting Corporation.

I write poetry because I can't help writing it. It seems to be in my nature. When I was about twelve some thoughts came into my head one day and I felt compelled to put them down on a piece of paper. I knew what a poem was supposed to be because I had learned about it in school but it never occurred to me that I had written a poem. I continued writing poems every once in a while but I didn't tell anybody about it until I was nineteen or so. Then I showed a couple of my poems to a girl friend, and she showed them to somebody else, and that person showed them to the editor of a newspaper, and the editor printed them. The funny thing is that until I saw my poems in print I did not suspect that I was writing poetry even though by that time I had written more than a hundred poems. I wrote my poems because I couldn't help writing them, but I needed somebody else to tell me that this might eventually make me a poet.

Since that time I have written many more poems, and have published some in magazines, anthologies and books. Once I realized that I was going to be a writer of poems all my life I resolved to try to be a writer of good poems and learn all I possibly could about the craft of writing poetry, which includes a lot of other things, such as history, and language, and what goes on in other people's heads and in my own. I haven't finished learning all this, and of course I never will.

BROAD STREET, NEW YORK

In such a manner might
the momentum of our mistakes
carry us down
the humourless drain of history.

My 23rd floor lawyer
looking in the cold morning light
at a quarter of a million
dollars worth of worthless
pre-war bonds & stocks
and being optimistic.

Planners drill
                        tunnels
raise   towers, monuments   design
                        parks
erect   structures of permanence   but
this is no city
no century for planners.

Except as these
clouds are perfect for soaring
this night
perfect for darkness
these streets are
perfect for kisses and for knives
nothing else.

What kind of practical men
buy and sell their stocks here in a dream?
What hopeful barristers invoke
what law?
Fingers of concrete question
a capricious sky.

Cautious downtown
                emptied
by long silent rails for the night
of briefcases, aspirins and
the subway faces of defeat
                where
do the elect live whose malice could injure
whose goodwill could bind
this wounded, patient world
                      and how far
will these granite blocks be flung
by a single pelvic thrust of time?

Broad Street opens into Wall Street in downtown Manhattan, and Wall Street is the centre of the financial district in New York. I spent a morning with a lawyer on Broad Street, not a very long time ago, looking at some stocks and securities that the lawyer felt might be worth something, and I thought were worth nothing. However, they used to be worth quite a bit at one time, and people put money and hope in them, and believed in them, and thought they would retain their value forever. All this made me think of the things that I, or the lawyer, or the many people rushing around New York or Toronto trust and believe in right now, and how all these things may lose their value one day. But I'm expressing this much better in the poem.

HOTEL ROYAL, BUDAPEST

The April wind is gentle.
The socialist sky is blue.
Our limousine is waiting.

My friend the film director pans toward me

And stops with his innocent eyes in extreme close-up.
He informs me he's happy.

He is happy in a happy country
Free, creative, and soon he will drive
To his island retreat in his East German car.
He dollies back for a final goodby
And fades out slowly.

The April wind is gentle
The socialist sky is blue
The limousine waits patiently.

A shabby woman steps into the frame,
Informs me she has not eaten for three days
And asks me for five *forints*.

I wave at my friend and smile,
And give the woman three *forints*,
And get into my limousine.

They are probably both lying
And I've become too old to chase after
The whore of truth in strange cities.

Budapest is the city where I was born, and I was trying to register in this poem how strange my city seemed to me after an absence of a decade or so, and how the truth of her reality was like what used to be called a lady of easy virtue, giving herself to whomever offered more for her services. (I was also trying to describe a man by the words appropriate to his profession in the poem, and I think I succeeded.)

EMILE X, STUDENT REVOLUTIONARY, CITY HOSPITAL MORGUE, BUDAPEST

I

I'm a flame: a process not a structure.
Growing from match to paper to wall to roof
Growing from house to houses to street to town
I have shape, height and bulk only to deceive those
Who think they can know my limits.

I don't mean to boast: a child's breath blows me out
And I retreat hissing from a bucket of water;
But I won't be cut down to size, defined,
Contained, dismissed: I'm a flame, I'm alive,
I can't be measured in inches or weighed in carats,
I flare up or die down; celluloid
Transports me in a flash; oil
Feeds me; timber
Preserves me; I burn, therefore I am.

Of course I have often been harnessed
Ever since Prometheus, for I'm strong
Yet less trouble than elephants or horses,
And willing to serve for I'm above service;
Like all things, I don't know right from wrong
And I exist only to be, like all things.

Men have cursed me and worshipped me.
I have warmed them and I have killed them,
As I've warmed or killed their enemies.
No one has ever stopped me. If I'm stopped I disappear.
I go underground. Everything combustible
Hides me forever. I'm a flame:
A process not a structure.

II

I died (to use a conventional term)
At six this afternoon, of complications
After a steel fragment lodged in the left
Upper part of my lung. The grenade was fired
By an enemy of the revolution
Using a grenade launcher, late last night.
As it was dark and things were kind of confused
It is also possible that a friend of the revolution
Launched the actual grenade. I mention this in brackets:
Whoever pulled the trigger, I was killed
By the enemy.

I'm a flame: a process not a structure.
If you capture me you have to feed me,
If you let me free I look after myself.
Only an enemy of the revolution,
An unthinking, wishful pig
Would try to put me out with bullets or grenades.

III

I address these remarks to you because you are a friend
And have come to look at me in the City Hospital Morgue
Where like a long white flame with a purple tip
I'm going through the invisible motions of rigor mortis
And maybe only you know that I'm alive.

For a while I will sleep now as flames sleep
In solid blocks of wood, electric wires,
Plastic fibres and sheets of aluminum.
I will sleep as gasoline sleeps in steel barrels,
Dynamite sticks in warehouses, as sound sleeps
In jet engines, as thunder sleeps
In tumulescent clouds above the Great Lakes.

I will not be dismantled or put out: you know me,

I'm a flame: a process not a structure.
Growing from match to paper to wall to roof
Growing from house to houses to street to town
From good to better to bad to worse
From love to malice to pain to compassion
From peace to justice to injustice to war
I burn, for burning is my business.

I'm a flame: a process not a structure.
Are you going to Canada? I'll see you soon.

Why is the line "I'm a flame: a process not a structure" used five times in the poem?

This is one of those almost true poems. I used to know a boy named Emile, who would have been described by his friends as a revolutionary, and he died under circumstances almost identical to those parodied slightly in the poem; but of course I did not have a conversation with his corpse in the City Hospital Morgue. In the poem I liken him to a flame and I predict that he will spread to Canada, and I hope I'm wrong but I don't think so.

ON A STATE FUNERAL

The man who was lying in his coffin
May not have appreciated the thunder of cannons
He may not have liked
The volley fired by an Irish guard
The sight of rifles and bayonets
Lining the street along which his caisson would roll
May not have won his approval at all
He might even have shrunk away from them

With some understandable fear
No matter how courageous a man he had been.

For it is not entirely impossible
That he had in fact heard a sound
An incomprehensible and distant sound
Before a sudden and unexpected
And manifestly unfair
Vicious explosion in his head
Flung him far into the regions
Of immediate memories
Receding and reverberating
With brilliant circles in soft darkness
Where he shook hands with many people
But did not see anybody
And something was very unusual
And there was no one to explain it
And he concluded that it was a mistake
And waited for it to go away
And groped for something familiar
And may have found it after a while.

But that one sound remained
As no other sounds followed it, it remained
An ugly, ominous, sharp crack
He may not have wished to hear again.

We who are temporarily left behind
Should be more compassionate
We should not torture without a good reason
The frightened and lonely dead
A time will come when we ourselves
May wish to rest and forget
And we should not discharge a gun
To honour a man who was shot in the head.

After President John F. Kennedy was assassinated I was watching his funeral on television (along with nearly three-quarters of the total population of Canada and the United States). I may have been the only one of all those millions of people who winced when the soldiers raised and fired their rifles repeatedly to salute their late Commander-in-Chief. For me, rifles seemed to be the wrong note at the time, but I have thought about it since and I may have been mistaken. What do you think?

THE CIRCLE NARROWS

It is quite possible
That our common thoughts come to us from the sea
Our doubtful soul follows the herrings
And we all die after the 11 o'clock news
Still there is
A certain self which I for my part
Keep wrapped in tinfoil among my private papers.

I am less and less concerned
With a planet I share with Arabs and caterpillars
With a country I share with fellow motorists
With women who share me with film directors
And with a heart that after minor adjustments
Could be used by a customs officer.

The trips I will take from now on
Must only be a few inches in length.

What does the poet mean by his "comment" on this poem?

In this poem, which is really the closing part of my book-length poem called *The Happy Hungry Man,* I'm talking about the fact that I seem to have much in common even with those things or people I have nothing in common with. But the person with whom I have the most in common is myself, which is not as obvious when one thinks about it as it would appear when one doesn't.

FIVE STANZAS ON PERFECTION

I will not be reduced to what I am
For I cannot quite return to the sea.
But naked in a circle of strangers
I have only been afraid of myself.

I am a cloud: I rain for the same reason
A tree grows or a cat stalks a mouse.
A cockroach can explain nine-tenths of me.
The rest sent Buddha into the wilderness.

I may only have to cut out one very small part
To attain perfection either way.
I have been exploring myself with a knife
I can do no more for the best of my friends.

Not something simple, my limbs or my glands
(Cripples and eunuchs still have narrow lips)
Nor is it primeval selfishness alone:
I have seen women and even children weep.

But maybe an impalpable dark plane
Such as some sleep: no ripple, sight or sound
Or meeting myself very suddenly
In a little-known part of any town.

What is the meaning of the first two lines in the third stanza?

This poem (which is from my first book called *The Absolute Smile*) is my definition of the idea of perfection. There is no better way in which I could explain what the poem means, because if there were I would have used it in the poem. I think it is a good poem, and a good poem is the best way of saying something with words. Maybe you could say it even better with music, or with pictures, but you can't with words. There is no point in asking the poet to use other words to explain the poem, because if he had better words for expressing his feelings, or his thoughts, he would have used those words in the first place. A poem may still seem complicated or obscure but this is not because the poet wants it to be complicated or obscure, but because the thoughts or emotions he has (or wishes to inspire in others) are complex and cannot be expressed in a simpler way. For relative to the complexity of the things it wishes to express, a poem is always meant to be the clearest, simplest and most illuminating way of saying something.

Lionel Kearns

By the Light of the Silvery McLune: Media Parables, Poems, Signs, Gestures, and Other Assaults on the Interface *is the full title of Lionel Kearns' most recent book of poems. The poet was born in Nelson, British Columbia, in 1937 and educated at the University of British Columbia and the School of Oriental and African Studies in the University of London. While at U.B.C., he was active in the* Tish *group of West Coast writers. Two recent collections are* Pointing *and* By the Light, *etc. He teaches in the English Department of Simon Fraser University in Burnaby, British Columbia.*

I played hockey since I was eight years old, and blew jazz saxophone all through my teens. I did a lot of other things too, but these two activities served as the basic training for my later career as a poet. This is not as strange as it seems. Hockey and jazz both require preverbal response, as they are too fast for anything else. It's true that poetry is verbal, but the poet has to handle his material, language, in much the same way that a hockey player controls his body movements or a jazz musician manipulates his sound—that is, it's a matter of acting without the interference of forethought, of *expression* as a natural and spontaneous complement to *impression*. And of course it is always very honest, because if you are caught up in the experience of being yourself at any one instant and at the same time translating that experience into words, then there is just no time to be dishonest. If someone asks me why I write poems I say, "Because it's easier."

PRESENCE

Jolted
by an imagined
glimpse
of long
black hair

Or that
tingling
on my neck
like breath—

>   You
>   lurking
>   in the murky nowhere

>   Just beyond
>   my ragged rim
>   of light

What sort of experience would lead a poet to write this poem?

This is one of the first poems that I ever got published, and one of the few very early poems that I still like. It's a bit sentimental I guess, but still it has a kind of formal excellence. Read it aloud. Listen to the patterns of vowels and consonants. The images too are clean and distinctive. Strangely enough the experience out of which it was written is almost lost to me now, but there's the poem, as sound and healthy as the day it was born, and that is a quality of a good poem—it lasts.

IT

The inane
justice
of gratuitous
insanity
the poem

Crashes down
during the night
of the big wind

And is discovered
next morning
among fallen branches
and other debris

A thing
apart

    To be used
    or discarded

    Or kept on the mantel
    as decoration

    Or thrown into the fire

Poems occur all the time, and they occur to everyone. What distinguishes a poet, however, is his habit of being ready and waiting when the event takes place. The poet is always listening to the murmurings of his inner ear or considering the strange words that take form at the end of his pen, so that when the poem comes zooming in he can get it down in his notebook before it gets away.

FRIDAY AT THE EX

His beard
knotted
in a make-shift
loin-cloth

His arms
around a sagging
cardboard box
half-filled
with cake-mix samples
and raffle-slips
from hearing-aid firms

He stumbles
over empty bottles
apple-cores
and crumpled
program leaves—

An escapee
from the Shrine Circus

As the Whip cracks
The Zoomo-Plane
takes people up
and the Snake gives them
six minute thrills
he whispers:

"This midway
isn't licensed for wine
but they can spin candy
out of flesh"

Lionel Kearns

And goes on
tossing hoops
at kewpie dolls
and panda bears

Now he crosses
his legs
in full lotus

Just behind
the Crown & Anchor stand

Where agents display
thirty brands
of silver-base
deodorant

And pitchmen
ramble in their stalls
about a fountain-pen
that writes on walls

But the crowd
from the Fun-House
kick him and jeer

Though the star contortionist
(having always been good
at guessing weight)
pivots on one
pointed breast

And wipes
her eyes
with her tattooed
heels

While the sky
streaks red
above the row
of floodlights

And they jostle him
up the hill towards
the three ferris wheels

The Christ image dominates the poem. Trace the manifestations of this image in the poem from the title to the last three lines. Is the poet's use of the image always effective?

This is an old poem, written at a time when I was struggling to come to terms with my own Catholic background and upbringing. There were periods in my life when I seriously considered becoming a priest—a Benedictine perhaps, or maybe a Trappist Monk. Later my attitude changed drastically, but one of the consequences of the conflict was a series of poems, written over a period of some years, which dealt, one way or another, with the idea of Christ the crucified man, the archetypal martyr, or, as old Father Gallary used to say, the Divine Victim. Then one day I recognized Jesus in the crowd at the Pacific National Exhibition. And let me remind you that this took place quite some time ago when it was very rare to see someone with a beard and long hair and sandals and a robe. I'm not sure whether he had a crown of thorns or not, but he was walking around the fair taking it all in with a very concerned look on his face. That image stayed in my head for more than a year, in fact, until Easter Sunday when strangely enough I was attending Mass way out in East End Vancouver in a church beside a school called, appropriately, "Our Lady of Sorrows," for it was the very place where I had been traumatized for six months at the age of seven by vicious strap-wielding nuns. So there I was, a great many years later, in the same vicinity, thinking about what I had seen the previous summer at the PNE, when I was zonked with the poem. I whipped out my note book quick and wrote it down in much the same version as that presented here.

BLEEDING POEM

Bleeding in Patzcuaro
    with freezing moon and bitter *pulque*

Bleeding on streets
    in *cantinas*
    into my bowl of market-place *mole*

Bleeding in the launch on black Lake Patzcuaro

    Bleeding to Janitzio Island
with Morelos Colossus
and candied masks of Father Death
    and sputtering candles
    melting on tops of elaborate tombs

Bleeding amongst the ragged Tarascans
kneeling there in their old *serapes* and straw hats
    and there will be another basket-ball game
immediately after the Dance of the Moros

    Three Indians in stupid-face
with traditional butterfly fish-nets
      hopping about

There is no music
    MC on malfunctioning PA
      is trying to imitate Augustine Lara:
        Rosa/La mas hermosa...etc....

    Everybody Laughs
except old Morelos, revolutionary *bandido,* and now
    awesome witness of lake and island
standing stoney-cold and high into the blackness

       his immense feet
   almost the size of the basket-ball court

     Unseen in the background
this figure present and silently brooding on death himself
    the sacrificial death of violent uprisings
  and more the eternal Indian death
      of generations of fathers and children

Here the communicants
and me bleeding among crowds of watchers and waiters
    shivering under the clank of chapel Mass-bell
      trying to recall
    the black-snatched *putas* of Morelia
who wouldn't participate past their duty

      Thinking more the lying travel-ads
    the misleading local propaganda
and how we are presently standing here
  in the deathly cold of the Day of the Dead
at night, with no boats
     running back to the mainland for our price

But wait till the Indians bring out their grave-juice
(though you have to know the secret words in Tarascan)
    everybody laughs, the priest
      is Augustine Lara: *Rosa*...clank clank...

    But shouldn't we climb the hill
      and read the graffiti
        scratched on the end of Morelo's big toe?
no, someone will take our place if we move

Bleeding bleeding bleeding
        how long will we have to wait?

         when will the dead arrive
          when will we eat?

    Licorice bats and sugar frosted skeletons
whole edible altars with icing lace and taffy chalice
            a tin for the tourist coin

The paralyzed girl on the litter makes no noise
          the other children are trying to cry
                    no one puts in any money

              Bleeding family members
are waiting for their dead fathers. Everybody laughs
        there are also many smaller coffins
            some are the size of infants and babes
        some are made of candy

There are too many tourists
          there is not enough money
     Senor, there is not enough money, my wife is sick
            see how many of my little ones
                    are gone already

            But we will have them back tonight
that is why everyone is happy
          it is the night of the Day of the Dead
          it is too cold for guitars
                    the fishing is very poor

O drink the bitter *pulque* with the orange caterpillar

Eat the bleeding caterpillar in the freezing *mezcal*

O ghostly blood of the bottled worm

The devil worm in the Blakeian night of old cold Mexico

Where they are making it into a movie

        It's a kind of travelogue
            and I am bleeding with cold
but why are three of them in top hats
      and that other thin-nosed bastard in a kilt?
nobody looks at him

        Praying Tarascans and fantastic tombs
sometimes they light fresh candles
      on candied shrines of skull and crucifix
the camera crew stepping on them
      the director shouting
          moving them out of the way

        Floodlights freeze the kneeling children
GET OUT OF THE WAY
      some cannot understand Spanish
it is very cold and bleeding
      nobody laughs but the cast
          because it's in the script

They must shoot that sequence over again
          walking down from behind the rock
    making their way between flickering candles
        and entranced families

  the girl in the bikini shivers
under her fur coat. I am bleeding. Augustine Lara
     has been frozen into a pillar of salt
the dead are arriving now

Everybody is eating

     death dolls and candied corpses. Oh stop
oh frozen blood on Janitzio stone
  the secret grave juice, the sacred mushroom
     the ravaging spirits
of dead fathers and lost brothers
the drying fish-nets
    the wrinkled Tarascan faces
This is the night the dead are with us
     this is the feast of All Souls
  and I alone have nothing to eat

This is the night the sweet-tooth phantoms
    arrive in town for late dinner

Here is a meal
  prepared on bleak Janitzio Island
    by dying Indians and bleeding watchers

Here you can relish a candied death
    and Tarascan basket-ball

Here they are making it into a film

See the happy motor-launch owners of Patzcuaro

See the serapes stiff in the frozen dawn

The earth drinks up the death-chill blood

See how it drops and clots in the water

I have left my mark on the boat

The following afternoon we returned to the Capital. The mountain slopes were covered with flowering yellow bushes and the sun was so hot that we stopped to bathe in a waterfall by the side of the road. At dusk we came in sight of the city, the lights spread out below us twinkling for miles across the valley. When we arrived there was still time to get a shot of Vitamin K to stop the bleeding.

Does the poet's comment on the poem help to explain the title? How significant, and how effective, is the title?

This is a Halloween poem. It derives from an experience I had in Mexico many years ago when I went with several friends to witness the Day of the Dead celebrations of the Tarascan Indians on a little Island called Janitzio in the middle of Lake Patzcuaro. The island is a prominent landmark in the area, being visible for miles around the lake because of a huge monolithic statue of Morelos, one of the guerilla heroes of the Mexican revolution, that dominates the island's crown. On the shore of the island live the impoverished Tarascan fishermen, who tolerate the intrusion of outsiders into their sacred ceremony simply because they cannot afford to keep them out, though the Indians themselves make very little attempt to exploit the situation commercially. The spectacle was bizarre and a little disconcerting, with the Indian families sitting around with all their prepared food and delicacies which they would share with the spirits of their departed relatives, and the tourists, mostly Mexican, milling about, trying to keep warm and get a glimpse of what was supposed to happen. To complicate the whole business a Mexican film crew moved in and tried to shoot a scripted film using the crowd and the Indian ceremonies as background. Traditionally the Indians are supposed to share a specially brewed liquor with the watchers, but as far as I know they didn't on this occasion. We were a bit tipsy anyway, at least when we arrived, but as the night wore on we became numb with the cold. To make matters worse, my nose had begun to bleed earlier in the day, and this continued all night and into the next day. The poem spans about twenty-four hours, from dusk to dusk, during which time I did not sleep. It was not what I would call a particularly pleasant period in my life, yet it proved to have a profound effect, the details remaining vivid in my memory. Some years afterwards the whole thing suddenly came back to me, with everything snapping into place and making sense. I sat down and wrote it out as an episode in a long prose poetry sequence called *Listen George*, addressed to my friend George Bowering. Later I made minor alterations to the original text, and also divided it into lines. I think it is one of the best poems I have ever written.

FOREIGN AID

Relaxing all day in this tropical atmosphere
glass in hand, a mosquito net and fans at night
sweating a bit but never exerting yourself
you think how easy it would be to make it permanent

to become the modern counterpart of the old white planter.
You've met a few of them, no pith helmets now but
they still observe the decencies, dressing for dinner
playing bridge down at the Yacht Club, having cocktails

with our new High Commissioner. Perhaps you could manage it
as an oil-field specialist or missile tracking technician
British or American, even a Canadian might fit in
as bank manager or some kind of Foreign Aid expert

living on a small portion of your Canadian salary
with four servants and two cars and a house high on the hill
with a sea breeze and white neighbours. What if the wife
flies to New York every few months and the cost

of educating the children is ridiculous, at least
you're still enjoying good liquor and imported food
and in moments of privacy you relish the view
of the young servant on her knees scrubbing the floor

a wonderful creature really, strong, pretty and always cheerful.
Yes they've asked you to be god-father to her second child
and you're so delighted you raise her wages to $40 a month
Oh it's good to be good and still live the good life

and though your face grows redder and redder each year
(because after all a man would be mad to leave all this)
and though your body gets flabbier and you lose your hair
and your paunch sticks out above your khaki shorts, at least

the skin under your clothes seems to be turning even whiter
and you joke about this when you have guests visiting from home
and you're pointing out the interesting features of the local scene
the quaint behaviour, for example, of the native population

their innate laziness and lack of initiative, but they're
a happy lot generally. And finally, after years and years
of this pleasant life (and you're still an amiable chap yourself)
quite suddenly, as you are sleeping comfortably

(because of course your bedroom has air conditioning)
you open your eyes in total amazement
in time to meet death in the blackness
on the chopping blades of numberless machetes

Some time ago I spent a year in Trinidad. Until that time I had been pretty smug with the thought that Canada had no imperial intentions. Yet, here on this forgotten Caribbean island I saw the embryo of Canada's first colony. Rich, white Canadians swaggered around with an arrogant air of superiority and benign condescension that I had previously recognised as the characteristic behaviour only of Englishmen and Americans. I was disgusted and ashamed. I wrote this poem in 1965. In 1970, black mobs stoned the banks in Port-of-Spain. They were all Canadian-owned.

TELEPHONE

After completing his call
    Roderick discovered
  the phone-booth had no door
He was sure the door had been there
    when he entered
but there was no mistaking the fact
    that there was no door now

"Strange"
>	he thought to himself
as he examined the ceiling and floor
>	for a secret panel
>		or emergency exit-hatch
but after going over
>	the whole compartment
with infinite care and attention
he resigned himself to the idea
>		that he would be there
>	for a long time
>		if not indefinitely

In the heat of his first panic
>	Roderick phoned all his friends
>	telling them
>	what had happened
>	and asking for advice
>		They all thought
>	it was the funniest story
>	they'd ever heard
>	over a telephone
and they said "Yeah Roderick
>	that's a good one hohoho
HOHOHO we'll be right down
>	with a wrecking team
>		to get you out"
and one of them even suggested
>	that Roderick listen
>	to his new record
>	"I'll blow your mind
>	right out of that cubicle"
>		he said
>	but it didn't work
and they never came down
>	and soon Roderick
>		had used up
all the change in his pocket

and after that
        he could only make
                long-distance calls
   and reverse the charges
but because his long-distance friends
               were too far away
   they couldn't help him either
and soon they began to catch on
        to what he was up to
so they stopped accepting
          the charges
having realized that Roderick
   never sent them any money
          to cover the bills

   Of course Roderick
tried to communicate directly
      with people
         on the outside
  but these efforts
     as one might expect
proved utterly futile
   He would tap on the glass
      with his bare knuckles
but passers-by would either
    pretend to ignore him or just
      hurry on their way
going to the office weekdays
            or perhaps church
    Sunday mornings
though some of them
    became so accustomed to seeing
      Roderick in the same place
         day after day
that they grew somewhat familiar
and would even nod a quick hello
     if there was time
  or smile and wave good-morning

>Roderick
>>in his desperation
>found the one person
>>he could actually talk to
>>was the directory girl
>who answered when he dialed *Information*
>>the only number
>>>that could be reached
>>without first inserting a coin
>and he would talk to her
>>whenever he could
>>him making up names
>with problematical addresses
>>and then attempting
>>to talk about the weather
>or otherwise pleasantly
>>pass the time of day
>>while she searched her lists
>>>and apologized
>>>for taking so much time
>and gradually over the years
>>their relationship developed
>>>and he would repeat
>the same old cliché that she
>>was all the world to him
>which in Roderick's case
>>was the truth

>>However
>from time to time Roderick
>>found this *information* girl
>something less than perfect
>>for she tended to be jealous
>>>and would accuse him
>of chatting up the regular operators
>>or of having secret dealings
>>>with the boys
>>>in the service department

62 *Rhymes and Reasons*

all of which was quite impossible
   for the service department
      never answers its calls
and the regular girls
    are allowed to say only
      "Number please"
      "I beg your pardon"
      "Thank you" and
      "Please hold the line"
    this last phrase being
  particularly abhorrent to Roderick
but nevertheless she would accuse him
  of this kind of indiscretion
and he would get excited and scream
     "You stupid bitch you don't
understand! You don't understand!"
and she would start to cry
     and say "Roderick"
I've told you before
if you use that kind of language
    I'll never speak to you again"

  And she didn't
and this left Roderick
    counting his heartbeats
      hearing himself
    murmur and breathe
  with no one to talk to him
no one to lend an ear in response

And as Roderick's phone-booth
    gradually filled up
   with beard and excrement
shrubs and ivy
  grew up and obscured it
    from the outside
  so that today

no one knows whether Roderick
         is living or dead

Has this poem more than an autobiographical relevance? Is it really a comment on modern society?

This poem is a media parable, one of a series of narrative fantasies that I wrote in the late sixties in response to the ideas of Marshall McLuhan. It is also, in many respects, autobiographical.

Gwendolyn MacEwen

"The search for a reality which resolves all contradictions" is how Gwendolyn MacEwen once defined her poetic aim. The poet was born in Toronto in 1941 and dropped out of high school to complete her private studies in Middle Eastern history and culture. Two recent books of poems are A Breakfast for Barbarians *and* The Shadow-Maker *(which won for her the Governor General's Award in 1970). She has written two mystical novels,* Julian the Magician *and* The Twelve Circles of the Night. *Gwendolyn MacEwen is a freelance writer who supports herself through radio writing and poetry readings.*

In my poetry I am concerned with finding the relationships between what we call the "real" world and that other world which consists of dream, fantasy and myth. I've never felt that these "two worlds" are as separate as one might think, and in fact my poetry as well as my life seems to occupy a place—you might call it a kind of no-man's land—between the two. Very often experiences or observations which are immediate take on grand or universal significance for me, because they seem to capsulize and give new force to the age-old wonders, mysteries and fears which have always delighted and bewildered mankind. In my attempt to describe a world which is for me both miraculous and terrible, I make abundant use of myth, metaphor and symbol; these are as much a part of my language as the alphabet I use.

YOU HELD OUT THE LIGHT

You held out the light to light my cigarette
But when I leaned down to the flame
It singed my eyebrows and my hair;
Now it is always the same – no matter where
We meet, you burn me.
I must always stop and rub my eyes
And beat the living fire from my hair.

Apart from being a good example of why one should give up cigarettes, this poem attempts to make use of a very trivial experience in order to bring out the burning or blinding nature of an encounter between two people. At first the fire is just a match-flame, but by the end of the poem we have another kind of fire.

MANZINI: ESCAPE ARTIST

now there are no bonds except the flesh; listen—
there was this boy, Manzini, stubborn with
gut, stood with black tights and a turquoise
leaf across his sex

and smirking while the big
brute tied his neck arms legs, Manzini
naked waist up and white with sweat

struggled. Silent, delinquent, he
was suddenly all teeth and knee, straining slack
and excellent with sweat, inwardly

wondering if Houdini would take as long
as he; fighting time and the drenched
muscular ropes, as though his tendons were worn
on the outside—

as though his own guts were the ropes
encircling him; it was beautiful; it was thursday; listen—
there was this boy, Manzini

finally free, slid as snake from
his own sweet agonized skin, to throw his entrails
white upon the floor
with a cry of victory—

now there are no bonds except the flesh,
but listen, it was thursday, there was this boy,
Manzini—

This poem appears to move in a circular fashion. The last stanza takes the reader to the beginning of the poem again. Has this movement any allegorical significance? Compare the movement of this poem with J. Michael Yates' "In the blood-coloured cage."

Magicians, jugglers, trapeze artists, escape artists, are fascinating figures to me, for in their strange arts they seem to give expression to some very fundamental truths. The performance of a "Houdini," for instance, seems to me to be a wonderful allegory of the human struggle to achieve perfect freedom. But then if I were earning a living that way, I'd probably say it was just another job.

Gwendolyn MacEwen

WHEN I THINK ABOUT IT

when I think about it I know
with clear and terrible logic
that I have taken my life in my hands
everyday for almost thirty years,
what with drunken drivers, slippery
streets, lightning bolts, subway
trains, elevators, airplanes,
manholes, fences that can elec-
trocute you in a minute, falling
wires, high winds, floods, fires,
and when I think about it
my death and yours is everywhere
and I wonder if I am alive
by some sheer *fluke*,
or if the amazing thing is
not that accidents happen
but that sometimes they *don't*
in view of the million possibilities.
and when I think about it
everything becomes impossible,
getting across the street
is a major challenge, I take nothing
for granted, knowing I have earned
this minute by a series
of incredible stunts and manoeuvres
which, when I think about them
require ever more time and energy
till there's little left
for anything else,
and when I think about it
I am an animal fighting
against desperate odds for sheer
survival (it starts to show
in my eyes), and when others are bored
because nothing is *happening*, I'm

on my knees thanking God that nothing
is happening, that the mad cab driver
didn't smear us all over the street,
that the plane for some incredible reason
stayed up and kept on flying.
and when I think about it
I don't know how I came this far,
or how much farther this wild luck will prevail,
or how I made it up to now, alive,
to tell the tale.

All I can say about this poem is that I'm trying not to think about it.

MEDITATIONS OF A SEAMSTRESS (1)

When it's all too much to handle
and the green seams of the world start fraying,
I drink white wine and sew
like it was going out of style;
      curtains become dresses, dresses
become pillowcovers, clothes
I've worn forever get taken in or out.
Now I can't explain exactly
what comes over me, but when the phone rings
I tell people I'm indisposed;
I refuse to answer the door, I even
neglect my mail.
      (Something vital is at stake,
The Lost Stitch or the Ultimate Armhole,
I don't know what) and hour after hour
on the venerable Singer

I make strong strong seams for my dresses
and my world.
      The wine possesses me
and I sew like a fiend, forgetting to use
the right colours of thread, unable to make
a single straight line;
I know somehow I'm fighting time
and if it's not all done by nightfall
everything will come apart again;
continental shelves will slowly drift into the sea
and earthquakes will tear wide open
the worn-out patches of Asia.

Dusk, a dark needle, stabs the city
and I get visions of chasing fiery spools of thread
mile after mile over highways and fields
until I inhabit some place at the hem of the world
where all the long blue draperies
of skies and rivers wind;
      spiders' webs describe
the circling of their frail thoughts forever;
everything fits at last and someone has lined
the thin fabric of this life I wear with grass.

This poem wrote itself quite naturally, because I was not striving for any particular effect other than the central idea of the "holding together" of things. If it's not all done by nightfall, everything will come apart again.

MEDITATIONS OF A SEAMSTRESS (2)

I dream impossible clothes which will confess me
and fall apart miraculous as the Red Sea

to reveal to you the stunning contours of my
mind, (you who wear the world with a grace
I will never achieve, invisibly,
like the arcane garment of the emperor).
I dream things not to be worn in this city,
yards of silks which like Isadora's scarf
may one day choke me, blue tunics held together
by buckles bearing the portraits of lost kings,
vests carved out of the skin of frightened deer,
green velvet cloaks in which I may soundlessly collapse
and succumb to the forest, sleeves to stress
the arm of the archer, the huntress, Artemis.

Only one dress I ever made came out right
(it will never happen that way again);
all the way down the front of it
where it opens from the collar to the hem
I sewed the signs of Athens,
a row of obsolete but perfect keys
on a strip of black and gold,
with which you may, O naked emperor,
enter and decode my world.

Clothes, like facial expressions, like words, can either conceal or reveal the character. In this poem I consider a series of possible outfits, none of which, however, can be worn with the grace and confidence with which the emperor of the famous children's tale wears his nakedness.

WRITTEN AFTER COMING OUT OF A DEEP SLEEP

How did I see the people of my dream when my eyes were closed?

Because you saw them with the eyes of your mind.

And now that I am awake do I see with my own eyes?

*No. You are the eyes of my Mind, and you are here
to help me see my Dream.*

Finally, who dreams who? Perhaps you are my dream, and I am yours, or perhaps we are all the dream of God.

Gwendolyn MacEwen says, "I make abundant use of myth, metaphor and symbol; these are as much a part of my language as the alphabet I use". Show the relevance of this statement to the poems Miss MacEwen has selected.

Tom Marshall

"*I am interested in what interests most writers,*" Tom Marshall writes, "*snow, sea-gulls, war, ancestors, sun, rain, motor-boats, ghosts, atoms.*" The poet was born at Niagara Falls in 1938 and graduated from Queen's University and the University of London. His first full-length book of poems is The Silences of Fire. *In addition to poetry, he has edited* A. M. Klein *(a critical work) and written* The Psychic Mariner *(a study of D. H. Lawrence's poems). He edits* Quarry *and, with David Helwig, has compiled a collection called* 14 Stories High.

I don't know if I know why I write poems. I don't think I ever had a choice. I think maybe you write poems to establish what is real. Maybe no experience is real (or fully realized as part of the whole universe) until you name it. Maybe you always falsify it (a little or a lot) when you do. (Because you fall in love with language, which is a world in itself.) Maybe then you have to do it over and over. Maybe there are worse ways to live. It isn't futile, I don't think, to attempt to discover the whole pattern of your experience—it is necessary for all of us to do so in some way. If artists are more disturbed than other people, they are also closer to the ground of our common and universal needs and thus closer to their resolution. Increasingly, I want to write something that reflects my sense of the ultimate unity of all things—both past and future, both what we call living and what we foolishly consider "inorganic." I want now to write out of ecstasy.

AUTOBIOGRAPHIES

I

I ate the mint-leaves among the railway cinders.
The sun flamed, at night the trains rumbled, the waterfall roared: the town splayed upon the terrible fountain.
On the air floats Ponce de Leon's gaudy illusion:
the fast cars, the fast girls who opened their legs,
drunk over the river, roaring in Buffalo,
stumbling over beer-cans on the midnight beaches.
In dreams I slid into the crashing waters
so easily, so easily I thought all waters
lived in my veins and flowed in living fountains.
The blackshirt hoods lounged sulkily on Centre St.,
dark guardians of human pain, warning angels
with truths too simple for the roaring boys.
The mirror of Narcissus lay hid in the wood
a dark enamelled pool flecked with angry stars.

II

The groundhogs nuzzling at the window-panes
in the brilliant moonlight have awakened me
from superb dreams of holocaust and retribution.
These brilliant, restless nights, the torments of hay-fever
exacerbate the itch in the shocked brain.
A woman sleeps, or does not sleep, in another room.
Her white hair electric, outspread, fills the moonlit windows,
she lies against the night and the angry stars
of ten, perhaps twenty years. An owl's cry
is all but lost in the reckless barrage of moonlight,
the loud torrent that breaks and conquers the grotesque shapes
of groundhogs, trees, badgers or whatever wakes.
The wood is lunatic, shaken with incandescent life.
In this house of illness, guilt and moonlight
I am pierced by the white, corrosive eye of God.

How does the last line of the poem relate to Part I?

"Autobiographies" was written in London, England, but concerns growing up in Niagara Falls, Ontario, and then, in Part II, coming back to visit after some years. As a child I ate the mint-leaves that grew by the railway tracks—they were magical, as were the falls themselves. Niagara Falls is both an over-grown village and a wild border-town full of the illusion of eternal youth and excitement. I thought of the falls then as Ponce de Leon's fountain of youth. Later, however, I hated the place, and when I visited my parents in their suburban home on the escarpment I woke up one night in the brilliant moonlight and was suddenly aware that death and its terror were the real end of the search for the fountain. My mother was at that time very ill. I wrote the poem six months later when I was at some distance of time and space from the experience.

WORDS IN EXILE

I

As the year
moves to its darkness, I move
walk, run, cross Russell Square
in the fugitive sunlight. Pigeons,
leaves are flying. Red hydrangeas
burn on the air. Glowing
coals of solstice. How your cheeks grew
hollow with dark
two years ago.

II

LONDON,

the great Beast. Paper
crackles in the flames, no sky, only white
Presence in the air. I walk
run, cross Russell Square
in the fugitive sunlight.
Think: Agincourt, the burgeoning earth inhabited
by many dead.

III

When my grand-
mother, ELLEN, was buried, not there
but at Niagara, the wind twisted the earth, stung
on the false face of grief. Leaves
rattled along the earth.

IV

The trees
in England are ghostly, behind the eyes
surpassing the moon. Whose white limbs
are theirs, her comeliness. Whose limbs
are white in a thin
drizzle of rain. Trees
are beautiful, and not dismayed
at mere human grief. They turn
on the air. They dance.

V

MATTHEW, my grand-
father died at 93. He did not dance. And if
he burned it was the cold burning of snow. He did not know
how to dance. And fire fell on him. His bones
burn in the burgeoning earth of Agincourt.

VI

And I
shivered that day, in sunlight, fugitive, I
whirling, a leaf caught, and carried to darkness, space, falling
outward from earth, from air, a black
desolate astronaut.

VII

Paper
crackles in the flames, no sky, only white
Presence in the air. Still the rain
holds off, and the humid square
smells like a lover's body. You
are living still. As the year.

VIII

Trees
are beautiful, and not dismayed. Pigeons,
leaves are flying. Red hydrangeas
burn on the air. I move
walk, run. In the white
Presence of the air. The humid square
smells like a lover's body. You
are living still
like a solstice coal.

Does it matter that the poet is not factually accurate? Does it matter that he continues to use the word "hydrangeas" instead of changing it to "geraniums"?

"Words in Exile" is a kind of circular meditation mixing memories and immediate sensations as certain films do. I used to walk across Russell Square every day to get to my work in the British Museum. With winter approaching, the London sun was intermittent if it appeared at all. At this point I hadn't yet come to love the place. I was lonely, and had gloomy poet's thoughts about death—about my grandparents' funerals (these grandparents were not, though it doesn't matter, from the same side of the family—I've also changed their names) and about the older Canadian world they lived in. I thought of my grandfather's funeral three months before in Agincourt (just out of Toronto, though you can think of the medieval battleground also, if you like). I had felt very strange. The ground was uneven, full of little clumps and hillocks. Lots of his and my relatives and ancestors were buried there. I had a fantasy that I had grown out of this earth but was now dangling in outer space from a long stem-lifeline. (This was before the film *2001*). There is something hallucinatory about the whole poem but it was all based on real experience, and no drugs were involved. (Two more things: [1] My mother says her father, a very stern puritan, was reputed to be quite a swinger before he married, so maybe he did dance. [2] Hydrangeas are always blue or pink —it was really geraniums that I saw. But I like the sound of "hydrangea.")

INTERIOR MONOLOGUE #666

> *Hydrocephalics are holy too,*
> *they have*
> *a certain*
> *bloated beatitude. . . .*

I think I am becoming
a tree. At any rate
something slow, lethargic,
vegetable. I am said
to resemble a rutabaga.

Do rutabagas have leaves
I wonder? I should like

to have leaves at least.
Slow ones. Leaves of pain
perhaps. Leaves of sleep.

It is said the gods
descend at last. In U.F.O.'s
perhaps. In B.V.D.'s for all
I care. Who cares if gods
descend? They are leaves

of sky, my leaves. Mine,
perhaps yours, I would be generous.
Every day the sky has leaves.
The sky-tree has grey leaves.
The sky-tree is ours.

This poem is even freakier than the last, I suppose. It was inspired by two jesting remarks of a friend—he said I had a fat head, that I must be a hydrocephalic, or maybe a rutabaga. The latter suggestion appealed to me a bit more since I've sometimes thought it would be nice to be a vegetable. I mean, to experience yourself and the environment very basically without thoughts, anxieties or emotions—as a tree does. I like trees. In Norse mythology the whole universe is a tree—Yggdrasil. Because we all grow together to something. I like this poem because it shows me in a happy mystical state.

RIDING IN COLIN'S BOAT (THE POETICS THEREOF)

Drunk, we slop and throb
on water. The boat
bends and sways about
crazily. The shoreline leans,
burns.

On the sky bobs
Christ the Astronaut.

>(we poets fink out
>of our unbearable visions
>observe now the birds
>of purgatory settle
>dull brown sea
>faces blank again

CHRIST THE ASTRONAUT

BURNS ON THE SKY

NAKED WITH LUST AND PAIN

Hold to it. Hold
to Christ the Astronaut.

>(now the place is reached

A reddish wake of sun
touches the drunken lake.
The motor cuts. The boat's
thrust and lurch give way.

The island of birds arises.

How is the poem changed if the poet's parenthetical remarks are ignored?

This is also a happy poem, I think. All I remember about writing it is that it went through a number of versions—this is unusual with me, I couldn't rewrite when I was younger and now, though the silences are longer, I usually get what I want right away. The occasion was a number of trips some of us took across Lake Ontario from Kingston to a partially submerged shelf of rock on Howe Island. We also buzzed the multitudinous birds settled on other, smaller islands. The boat was small and unstable, and thus more fun. As for Christ the Astronaut, he was originally the sun combined with some image of myself that was evolving. There are moments you can feel are paradise, whatever the pain before. (Like childbirth, or love, or arriving finally.) We all turn and return to some such island.

SONG

in chambers of spring
air and water
shimmer cool as cymbals

in chambers of spring
gown and curtain
ripple green as glass

in chambers of spring
moon and willow
waver pale as candles

in chambers of spring
fire and wind
mingle bright as beads

you who snared my love
in a smiling net of flame
come and lie with me
in the chambers of spring

you who caught my joy
tight in curls of cloudy gold
come and lie with me
in the chambers of spring

you who fixed desire fast
in eyes quivering arrow green
come and lie with me
in the chambers of spring

Why did the poet change the placement of the words "chambers of spring"?

This poem was originally written in midwinter almost ten years ago. I was in love at the time, of course. Or, at least, one little push would have done for me. That happened later, but everything was still potential when the poem was written. The immediate stimulus was a concert of chamber music in an oak-panelled room of the university's oldest women's residence. I don't remember who played, or what, but it moved me to write this poem. I think it was in February, when you imagine, absurdly, that spring is almost there.

WEST STREET

I woke up at midnight and heard him singing
the wooden owl above my balcony
at long last flying free
That owl-house my apartment was flying
the park outside singing in the midnight wind

Limestone and brickwork of Kingston made
a high sweet song
till midnight was noon and gold sun shining
tumult in the willows their gold whips turning
into a kind of singing

The owl fierce with midnight song
the gold willow singing in the wild sunshine
limestone and park singing
about stone and gardens that live forever
by noon and midnight

I wrote this poem late this fall during one day when I was, with a few friends, going out to visit Al Purdy at Roblin Lake. I wrote some before we left and the rest while we were out there. It was meant to be a song lyric that a student friend of mine could set to music, but I decided later that it wasn't too suitable for that. West Street is a Kingston street facing a beautiful park; I lived there for over two years. (Once, a ferocious faculty wife asked me what it was like to live in such a "student Bohemia.") Over my third-floor apartment's large front window was a brown owl facing the park. I thought he was wood (and said so in an earlier poem), but a friend, David Helwig, tapped him and discovered he was really painted tin. Later David, who is a writer, too, criticized me for calling the owl "wood" again, but I replied, "David, I've been an historian, and I know the difference." The owl is my bird, as the cat is my animal; I don't know why—they chose me. The willows are actually located by my present apartment. Interestingly enough, Al Purdy has very similar ones in front of his A-frame cottage. The poem expresses a new feeling of freedom—freedom is when you know a little better who you are, and like it.

John Newlove

"He continues to be autobiographical although his perspective transcends the purely subjective," Michael Gnarowski has written about the poetry of John Newlove. Born in Regina in 1938, the poet lived on the West Coast when the Tish group was active. He has published a number of books, especially Black Night Window and The Cave. He is the main contributor to Thumbprints, a collection of hitchhiking poems edited by Doug Fetherling. John Newlove now lives in Toronto and works in the world of publishing.

If anyone is interested in the relative ages of these pieces, they were written (with long gaps and other pieces between each) in this order: "Elephants," "By the Church Wall," "Ride off any Horizon," "She" and "Dream" (in roughly the same period, but with "She" beginning first and taking longer to finish), and "The Engine and the Sea."

BY THE CHURCH WALL

The mocking faces appear in the churchyard,
appear as I curl on the hard ground,
trying to sleep—trying to sleep
as the voices call me, asking why
must I always be frightened and dreaming?

I have travelled this road many times,
though not in this place, tired
in the bones and the long blistered feet,
beneath a black mass of flat clouds,
dry in a damned and useless land.

Frogs croak hollowly, the loons cry
their thin bewildered song on a far-off lake,
the wind rises and the wet grass waves;
by the wall of the white rural church
I count a thousand to go to sleep.

But it will not happen. The faces
float before me, bloated and grinning,
succubus and incubus, a child
screams in a house across the road;
I turn and turn in my fear.

There is nothing to hurt me here,
and I know it, but an ancient dread
clenches my belly and fluttering heart,
and in the cold wet grass I count
what may happen and what has.

All the mistakes and desires are here,
old nameless shame for my lies,
the boy's terrible desire to be good and

not to be alone, not to be alone,
to be loved and to love.

I remember a letter a friend sent,
trivial and gossiping, quite plain,
of no consequence to him, casually typed,
and then signed easily by hand,
All our love: and wish I could say that.

But I lie alone in the shadowed grass,
fond only, incapable of love or truth,
caught in all I have done, afraid
and unable to escape, formulating
one more ruinous way to safety.

In "By the Church Wall," there are repetitions of a sort I use often: "trying to sleep—trying to sleep," echoed by "not to be alone, not to be alone" in construction. I also like puns and near-puns; I have difficulty avoiding them, in fact. In the last line of stanza two, there is a punning with "damned," the other sound being, of course, "dammed," and the clue is given in the same line in the word "dry"—a dam may store water, but the places the water is taken from for storage will be left drier than they might have been before. In the last line of this piece, "one more ruinous way," the word "more" was used because it gives two readings, both of which I wanted, *i.e.*, "another ruinous way" and "a way that is even more ruinous than the others." It was my birthday, I was alone with an unknown country spread out around me, unknown people, and if I had ever felt suicidal this was the time. That feeling of complete despair somehow fostered a formality in me, perhaps the formal manners of a person who has no hope left, rather than a wildness. I had, then, given up too wholly to fight back.

SHE

She starts to grow tears, chemical beast
shut in a dark room with the walls closing
behind her eyelids, all touches hateful,
the white sweep of clean snow death to her,
the grey naked trees death to her.

Her face swells. Tears
slide like glycerine down the round cheeks
and shimmer on her chin. No motion
escapes her face; sadness gathers
in her bones; her fingers curl, an ulcer
pins her down, rotting in her body.

The quiet shadows on the screen
dance, gesticulate, the news comes on and goes,
cars are sold, women sing and smile,
but she does not. Still the tears
run down without a sound. She curls
on her couch; she moves a bit, moves heavily,
as if she had forgotten how to move.

She moves. The snow shines through the window,
a phosphorescent sea, gleaming;
the etched ghosts of the night sway slightly.

The grass is dead. In spring
it will not be the same, the trees
with their sticky shiny leaves will only be
in costume, mocking, the fresh air
will lie; animals stretching in their skins
stretch to die. But she moves.

She moves. Her shoulders ache. She feels
the harnesses she lives in, she feels

the jelly on her skeleton, she feels the tears
upon her face and dries them with her hands,
touches her hair, sits up and tries to smile.

It is a brave attempt, saying: See how brave I am!
Her breasts hang heavy on her, and the room is dark.

*The poet says, "Everything is filtered through a mind, hers and mine."
But is not the poem filtered solely through the poet's mind?*

"She" is as true as I can make it now. Sitting in the same room, watching, feeling my own (different) emotions, including despair and desire mixed, how could I ever say with accuracy *just* what she felt? But this was what seemed to be, and I had known her intensely for a long time. Parts of the piece may be a little obscure; I hope not. Everything is filtered through a mind, hers and mine, and the mind acts upon the world. "The etched ghosts of the night" were the trees outside the window; the phrase began quite differently, but as the poem was rewritten and rewritten it changed slowly under my hands to this.

THE ENGINE AND THE SEA

The locomotive in the city's distance, obscure, misplaced, sounds a child's horn on the flat land leading to the cliff of dark buildings,

the foghorns on the water's edge cry back.

Between the sounds men sit in their houses watching machines inform them in Edison's light. In the marshes, the music of ominous living...

a leggy insect runs on that surface, frogs wait, fish, angling birds.

In the cities men wait to be told. They sit between the locomotive and the fish. The flat sea and the prairie that was a sea contain them. Images float before their eyes,

men and women acting,

entertaining, rigorously dancing with fractured minds contorted to a joyless pleasure, time sold from life.

The locomotive hums, the prairies hum. Frogs touch insects with their long tongues, the cannibal fish and the stabbing birds

wait.

Night actions flash before uncountable animal eyes. Mice run. Light rain falls in the night.

The frogs are stilled. Between the engine and the sea, the lights go out. People sleep with mechanical dreams, the sea hums with rain, the locomotive shines black, fish wait under the surface of a pinked pool.

Frogs shiver in the cold. The land waits, black, dreaming. Men lie dry in their beds.

History, history!

Under the closed lids their eyes flick back and forth as they try to follow the frightening shapes of their desires.

How does the use of the word "wait" add to the ominous mood of the poem?

John Newlove

"The Engine and the Sea" also grew slowly. I wanted the longer rhythms and the slower cadences I thought this prose-like line would give me. I could not see why I should be restricted to the normal lengths of lines in poetry or to, say, the width of the page I worked upon, if neither would accomplish my purpose. After all, I was the maker; I was in charge here, hopefully, not past usage; we can do nothing with the past except endure its memory. The piece is a *mélange* of dream and drifting thought after the dream, of the south coast of British Columbia (an old locomotive engine, by the way, sits outside Kitsilano beach there, and I suppose some night it planted a visual seed in me) and a boyhood spent on the prairies, of reading about glacial ages and huge inland seas, watching swamp ponds and television, of men and engines and the land—and all of them seeming to me then to have lives of their own, real, sentient lives—inextricably mixed with each other; and of the horror of history, which to me is the story of human desires bloodily struggled for, not only bodies maimed but minds as well and whole continents too. Often I speak of desire: how much it is proper to wish to grasp, and the consequences.

RIDE OFF ANY HORIZON

Ride off any horizon
and let the measure fall
where it may—

on the hot wheat,
on the dark yellow fields
of wild mustard, the fields

of bad farmers, on the river,
on the dirty river full
of boys and the throbbing

powerhouse and the low dam
of cheap cement and rocks
boiling with white water,

and on the cows and their powerful
bulls, the heavy tracks
filling with liquid at the edge

of the narrow prairie
river running steadily away.

*

Ride off any horizon
and let the measure fall
where it may—

among the piles of bones
that dot the prairie

in vision and history
(the buffalo and deer,

dead indians, dead settlers,
the frames of lost houses

left behind in the dust
of the depression,

dry and profound, that
will come again in the land

and in the spirit, the land
shifting and the minds

blown dry and empty—
I have not seen it! except

in pictures and talk—
but there is the fence

covered with dust, laden,
the wrecked house stupidly empty)—

here is a picture for your wallet,
of the beaten farmer and his wife
leaning toward each other—

sadly smiling, and emptied of desire.

*

Ride off any horizon
and let the measure fall
where it may—

off the edge
of the black prairie

as you thought you could fall,
a boy at sunset

not watching the sun
set but watching the black earth,

never-ending they said in school,
round: but you saw it ending,

finished, definite, precise—
visible only miles away.

*

Ride off any horizon
and let the measure fall
where it may—

on a hot night the town
is in the streets—

the boys and girls
are practising against

each other, the men
talk and eye the girls—

the women talk and
eye each other, the indians
play pool: eye on the ball.

*

Ride off any horizon
and let the measure fall
where it may—

and damn the troops, the horsemen
are wheeling in the sunshine,
the cree, practising

their deaths: mr poundmaker,
gentle sweet mr bigbear,
it is not unfortunately

quite enough to be innocent,
it is not enough merely
not to offend—

at times to be born
is enough, to be
in the way is too much—

some colonel otter, some
major-general middleton will
get you, you—

indian. It is no good to say,
I would rather die
at once than be in that place—

though you love that land more,
you will go where they take you.

*

Ride off any horizon
and let the measure fall—

where it may;
it doesn't have to be

the prairie. It could be
the cold soul of the cities
blown empty by commerce

and desiring commerce
to fill up the emptiness.

The streets are full of people.

It is night, the lights
are on; the wind

blows as far as it may. The streets
are dark and full of people.

Their eyes are fixed as far as
they can see beyond each other—

to the concrete horizon, definite,
tall against the mountains,
stopping vision visibly.

The poem "also speaks of desire." What desire? Does it speak first of despair?

"Ride Off any Horizon" also speaks of desire, after the first section sets the place as the prairies I grew up on; it is difficult to tell, but the piece seems to be so plain that I cannot see any comment on it from me being useful.

DREAM

The lone figure leans in the snow.
A rifle is stuck beside him:
one hand is on it.

He waits an approaching figure.
He will decide, when it comes,
to kill or to run.

It is the white centre of the world
his reason squats in.

"Dream" is, was, a dream. There was only the picture, bare, soundless, without motion except for the approaching dot near the white horizon. I do not know if I was the figure in the centre: half him, half not-him, both observer and the observed. But it was not so much the figure that was observed as the emotion. "Apprehension," among other things, can mean both "understanding" and "dread"; it is a coupling that fascinates me. The indecisive apprehension felt in the dream seemed real; the figure's mind trembled as a frightened animal would, but as the emotion slowly gelled into terror it was not clear whether flight or murder would be the result. Both seemed possible. There was only stillness, only that single point in the middle of a world as blank as a remote planet made of perfectly polished steel, with the unknown approaching.

ELEPHANTS

aren't any more important
than insects,

but I'm on the side
of elephants,

unless one of them tries
to crawl up my leg.

"Elephants" is simply a joke cadenced by phrases; a joke about my paranoia, one of those exaggerations that seem to indicate the truth better than a precise telling of it could; a denigrating badge worn for the sake of identification.

Alden Nowlan

"*Concise, realistic, and often bitterly ironic*"—*these are the adjectives chosen by A. J. M. Smith to describe the poems of Alden Nowlan. The poet was born in Windsor, Nova Scotia, in 1933, and worked as news editor of* The Telegraph-Journal *in Saint John. He has published a book of stories,* Miracle at Indian River, *and his book of verse,* Bread, Wine and Salt, *earned him the Governor General's Award in 1969. Alden Nowlan is Writer in Residence at the University of New Brunswick, Fredericton.*

I write for the same reason I'm six feet, three inches tall: I can't help it. I began writing stories and poems when I was eleven years old and am still at it twenty-six years later. For me, writing has come to consist of discovery, organization and incantation, although not everything I write involves all three of those processes. Sometimes I think of myself as an explorer of an interior landscape: the poems that I find most satisfying are those that give form to some discovery I've made about myself and, through myself, about others. "On the Nature of Human Compassion" is that kind of poem. Then again, sometimes I think of the poet as a kind of magician. "I, Icarus" and "Alpha and Omega" are examples of what I consider magical poems—poems that attempt to express the infinite strangeness of our ordinary lives. There are even moments when I think of the poet as a drudge; because, among other things, writing poetry is hard work, and the longer you keep at it the harder it gets. Poetry, to me, is communication, although I'm not always certain to whom the communication is addressed. Perhaps to God. Perhaps to an ideal listener. Perhaps, and I suspect this is nearest the truth in my own case, to an imaginary playmate. I also believe that the reader—the sympathetic and intelligent reader—shares in the creation of the poem. So when you read my verses you're helping to create them. Thank you.

THE EXECUTION

On the night of the execution
a man at the door
mistook me for the coroner.
"Press," I said.

But he didn't understand. He led me
into the wrong room
where the sheriff greeted me:
"You're late, Padre."

"You're wrong," I told him. "I'm Press."
"Yes of course, Reverend Press."
We went down a stairway.

"Ah, Mr. Ellis," said the Deputy.
"Press!" I shouted. But he shoved me
through a black curtain.
The lights were so bright
I couldn't see the faces
of the men sitting
opposite. But, thank God, I thought
they can see me!

"Look!" I cried. "Look at my face!
Doesn't any body know me?"

Then a hood covered my head.
"Don't make it harder for us," the hangman whispered.

As a newspaper reporter I talked with a number of men who had been sentenced to death. In every case the sentence was later commuted, but in one instance the gallows had already been built. It wasn't anything at all like scaffolds you've seen in films: towering structures with the legendary thirteen steps. It had been built in the basement of the jail, and they'd had to dig a pit in the floor to ensure that the drop would be long enough. There was a chair in case the victim wasn't able to stand up. But this poem, "The Execution," is a straight-forward account of a nightmare. The nightmare was exactly as I've described it; I simply woke up and wrote it down, without revising a line.

THE BULL MOOSE

Down from the purple mist of trees on the mountain,
lurching through forests of white spruce and cedar,
stumbling through tamarack swamps,
came the bull moose
to be stopped at last by a pole-fenced pasture.

Too tired to turn or, perhaps, aware
there was no place left to go, he stood with the cattle.
They, scenting the musk of death, seeing his great head
like the ritual mask of blood god, moved to the other end of
the field, and waited.

The neighbours heard of it, and by afternoon
cars lined the road. The children teased him
with alder switches and he gazed at them
like an old, tolerant collie. The woman asked
if he could have escaped from a Fair.
The oldest man in the parish remembered seeing
a gelded moose yoked with an ox for plowing.
The young men snickered and tried to pour beer
down his throat, while their girl friends took their pictures.

And the bull moose let them stroke his tick-ravaged flanks,
let them pry open his jaws with bottles, let a giggling girl

plant a little purple cap
of thistles on his head.
When the wardens came, everyone agreed it was a shame
to shoot anything so shaggy and cuddlesome.
He looked like the kind of pet
women put to bed with their sons.

So they held their fire. But just as the sun dropped in the river
the bull moose gathered his strength
like a scaffolded king, straightened and lifted his horns
so that even the wardens backed away as they raised their rifles.

When he roared, people ran to their cars. All the young men
leaned on their automobile horns as he toppled.

How does the poet encourage the reader to share in the creation of the poem? Does Nowlan use the same technique in "The Execution"?

Of all my poems, "The Bull Moose" has been anthologized most often. That, coupled with the fact that I wrote it quite a number of years ago, has put a certain distance between me and it, so that now when I look at it, it's almost as though I were looking at a poem written by somebody else. The poem was based on an actual incident: a moose did wander out of the woods near the little town in northwestern New Brunswick where I then lived. In an attempt to express the terrible dignity of the animal—how it somehow seemed to triumph over the indignities to which it was subjected—I used the familiar symbols of Christ's crucifixion. But it's important to remember that this is essentially a poem about a moose and not a poem about Christ. Some readers have even pointed to symbolism of which I wasn't aware. For instance, one student wrote that "the pole-fenced pasture" represented Judas Iscariot. I don't think I intended it that way, but I'm willing to admit he may have been right. This poem also represented a new phase in my development. If I remember rightly, I rewrote it close to thirty times before I even began to be satisfied with it. Until then I hadn't known that poetry demanded not only inspiration, but hard work.

ON THE NATURE OF HUMAN COMPASSION

I said to a herring gull with a broken wing:
Bird, I am sad for you.
If I could make you trust me
I'd take you up in my hands,
carry you back to the city
and hire a veterinarian to heal you.
Or if my stomach were stronger
I'd use a stone or a club of driftwood
to shorten your death.
                    And the herring gull answered:
Man, you are not sad for me,
but for yourself, so great an egotist
you can put on the body of a bird
or play Mephistopheles to a housefly,
what you call your compassion the conceit
that all living things are Alden Nowlan in disguise.

I saw the herring gull that is the subject of "On the Nature of Human Compassion" out the car window one Sunday afternoon when my wife and young son and I were driving along the sea shore. The memory of the bird, and the guilty knowledge that I hadn't done anything to help it, depressed me all the rest of the day. I suppose this poem is partly an act of expiation. The Zen Buddhists say that the ego must swell until it fills the universe and then it will burst like a balloon. Perhaps it's important to remember that the herring gull isn't really talking to the poet: he's talking to himself.

ALPHA AND OMEGA

I am awake. I know where I am. I have a name and a history.
All this is happening in Trafalgar Square, but will go on happening

wherever I am until I die. I boast of nothing,
each one of these thousands has created me,
is, therefore, my god. I am nobody,
only a childish wonder at how mysterious it is
that I am looking out through the eyes
of a certain body and this body is alive,
here and now, in the thin English sunlight,
surrounded by pigeons, as though we were all saints,
staring up at Lord Nelson, who looks as if he were being shot into
    space,
eyeing the black and sinister taxis, the huge toy buses,
the young men arrayed like Janisaries
who have looted the palace of a foppish sultan,
the beautiful young women who do not dress but simply
    adorn their nakedness.
It is a Sunday afternoon in August, 1967,
and there are many other places I could be
but no one else can stand
exactly where I am standing
now, thinking of Van Gogh's Sunflowers,
almost the only picture
in that giant mausoleum to reach out
    and touch me.

Compare this poem with Tom Marshall's "Words in Exile."

"Alpha and Omega" attempts to express one of those mysterious times when you are suddenly aware of how strange it is simply to be alive in the world. This particular time I was standing in front of the National Gallery in London looking out at Trafalgar Square. A friend, the poet Dorothy Livesay, tells me the poem transfigures reality in the same manner as the paintings of Chagall. An earlier version contained a reference to St. Thomas Aquinas: it's said that when he came to Paris as a young man somebody asked him, "Who are you? What are you doing here?" and he spent the rest of his life trying to find the answers to those questions.

I, ICARUS

There was a time when I could fly. I swear it.
Perhaps, if I think hard for a moment, I can even tell you the year.
My room was on the ground floor at the rear of the house.
My bed faced a window.
Night after night I lay on my bed and willed myself to fly.
It was hard work, I can tell you.
Sometimes I lay perfectly still for an hour before I felt my body
    rising from the bed.
I rose slowly, slowly until I floated three or four feet above the
    floor.
Then, with a kind of swimming motion, I propelled myself toward
    the window.
Outside, I rose higher and higher, above the pasture fence, above
    the clothesline, above the dark, haunted trees beyond the
    pasture.
And, all the time, I heard the music of flutes.
It seemed the wind made this music.
And sometimes there were voices singing.

When I was about fourteen years old I frequently had fantasies in which I could fly—exactly like the narrator in "I, Icarus." In fact only my common sense prevents me from believing that I actually did fly: the fantasies were that vivid. A friend of mine who is a student of the occult tells me I was probably projecting my astral body; but I'm too much of a materialist to believe that. Still I think I'd believe that there was a time when I really and truly flew, if I hadn't been told all my life that such a thing is impossible.

WALKING TOWARD THE BUS STATION

The snowflakes are shaped like starfish
and almost as big
as humming birds.
                    But I have forgotten
the colour of your coat
although you walk beside me.
Already
           this is part
                         of the past,
imaginary.
              So our mouths say nothing.
There are witnesses
who would swear
they saw us now.
                   In reality
we are each of us elsewhere
and alone.
               I am watching
a bus leaving:
                 to board a bus
is to step from this world
                             to another,
a small and private
                       transfiguration.
Or I have prevailed
against the cosmological winds
                                 and you did not go:
that same afternoon
we boarded a plane
                      together.
We have grown old in Spain.
And nobody has ever been
so happy except
the most celebrated lovers
                             and they

only in the imaginations
of their more envious admirers.

Doubtless you too are setting out for some place
other than where we both seem to be going.

What are the key lines in the poem?

I think that "Walking Toward the Bus Station" is a very simple poem about a very complicated matter. At every moment of our waking experience our minds are full of a thousand and one impressions, sensations, reminiscences, expectations, hopes, fears. We live out whole lives while we're brushing our teeth. The man and the woman or the boy and the girl seem to be simply walking toward the bus station. In his mind, however, he has already seen her go—or perhaps she didn't go, perhaps they went away together, to Spain. And all the time they are simply walking together in the snow—at least that's how it would appear to an onlooker who, unlike the poet, could not see into their minds. The poet, of course, is a magician.

J. Michael Yates

"Arctic wilderness and electronic machinery." J. Michael Yates writes, "I'm interested in the fusion of those two extremes, if possible." Born in Fulton, Missouri, in 1938, the poet and writer was educated at the University of Kansas City and the University of Michigan. In 1966, he joined the Creative Writing Department of the University of British Columbia where he helped to edit Prism International *and* Contemporary Literature in Translation. *Two recent books are* Man in the Glass Octopus *(a volume of "fictions") and* The Great Bear Lake Meditations *(a cycle of prose poems). He has written many radio plays which have been broadcast in Canada and Europe. He recently decided to write full-time, and has moved his library and camera equipment to the Queen Charlotte Islands.*

Toward a Label for a Soup-can, or: How do I know what I think until I see what I say?

1. For me, an image is one of an infinite number of entrances into an arena where something ineffable is going on. If the thing I'm after were stateable, probably it would be better said in expository prose. The issues most often taken up by good poetry require use of the silences between and behind words. For this mode of communication, metaphor, and indirection are the best engines.

2. With each piece, I attempt to cause a structure, a system of images whose parts belong dissonantly to a whole whose meaning cannot be stated. I mean Stravinsky's dissonance. In the *Poetics of Music,* he suggests that dissonance is only a transitional element; consonance must be achieved one way or another—either in the instrumentation or in the ear of the listener. The latter is my way—to give the reader the "thing" I'm

talking about, frame by frame, and ask him to project it inside him in the manner that most entertains him. Different and isolate as each of us is, it seems the only honesty.

3. Ideally, fifteen readers will make fifteen very different (and fifteen equally justifiable) poems from a piece I have written. As I'm different from you at any moment, I differ from myself through successive moments—even the most familiar things change, with changes in the co-ordinates of consciousness and time. I couldn't possibly recreate the co-ordinates of consciousness that produced a given piece and thereby tell you what it means.

4. Ideally, a reader would come to a poem relaxed, with open consciousness, no preconceptions, nor suspicions that the poem is a locked door and someone somewhere—probably the treacherous bastard author—is hiding the key. The parts of a poem which persist inside a reader arrive there via personal correspondences. Exterior interpretations remain merely exterior. Belief in one's own associations is difficult, very difficult. But only those will translate the poem from "mine" to "yours."

5. Ideally, one would read a poem as if he were the first reader in history to read a poem—and as if no one on earth were reading a poem at that moment. Impossible. Necessary.

6. Ideally, I write as if no one has ever written a poem. As if no one is writing now. Ridiculous. Imperative.

7. "Understanding" is a sweet, vague Renaissance dream which never came true. According to me, poems are not to be understood, but responded to. Understanding promises universal truth. Naive. I'm a rare user and no pusher at all of either reality or its ism. I don't assume a "representative universe." As if one could come to an "understanding" about such things.

IN MEMORIAM: PETER PAUL FERSCH

Gelegenheitsgedicht

I

The black tree at the end of the road
Exclaims the last syllable of the last sentence.

The black tree at the terminus
Is the only part of my horizon
That doesn't retreat as I near.

My hands and head and legs
Magnetize toward it like compass needles
And my skin takes on the
Look and feel of wood, darkly-grained.

Now my parts belong to no whole;
My limbs only resemble parts of other things,
And the axe I've carried always
Has always been rusting.

The moon is a dark side
And a light side
And all the same moon:
A small circle of fraudulent light
In the long fraudulent dark.

II

Like a faraway locomotive, a wind
Begins through the high needles of the trees,
And in my listening the bold print
Of the landscape goes italic.

The hair on my unbarbered neck rises a little.
Somewhere the fur of a sunflower-grizzly
Is blowing. Between these two animals
Moves a message neither thought nor sent.

I was and I no longer am.
The history of one man is a history of the world.

III

And if I had noticed them
Building the walls, what are
The whining objections of one in the face
Of huge machinery and many million hands
Directed toward a single end?
I peer in—one could say "out"—at the construction.
Not even when I blink most violently
Does anyone notice my eye.

Death like:
>*the sound of an insect suffocating in a jar.*
>*the last pin-prick of light when the television is over.*
>*the end or beginning of a long rain.*
>*an erasure, filaments part paper and part eraser*
>*scattered in the shape of a man, then blown away.*

IV

I believe in gasoline.
But whether touch off
The gallon with a match
Or burn on drop by drop
In the forms of a fine machine.
It only matters now.

It was a matter of driving down
From the mountains where the clear streams began
Into the wide clean of the plain
And into the sepia skies of the city.
Darkness was always falling. And filthy rain.

V

The fist of living unclenches.
Souls of the suicides fill
The spaces among a V of geese
Going toward the poisoning grounds.

There was no time to remember to be my murderer.

Botulism in the entrails of the weather
Twists the clouds and color of sky
In the motions of a fish strangling in air.

I'd always been gathering breath for the last thing to say.

Spring, then—a mote in the ray of dying.

Dust. Surprisingly, we were all made of almost all water.
Except for the dust. Beauty was water, brain was water,

But something was always dust clinging to the shine
Of a piano-top and cataracting the windows.

VI

The voice the other side of the glass
Is the soft mouth of a scavenger fish
Moving behind the aquarium-wall,

The no-voice, the silence after sound,
The silence forever thereafter.

*I could dream wars more terrible
Than history shall ever deliver.*

*The dream and the real wars are over.
I have won or lost or neither.*

*General Patton and Johann Bach
Are dancing among the children.*

VII

In the black tree at the end of the road,
A golden pheasant and a crow are mating.
Their ugly voices merge into a sound
Which is not unpleasant,
But the sun cannot pierce the branches
And the tree gives no shadow at any time of day.

Tennyson's In Memoriam expresses the poet's despair and perplexity at the death of a friend and his struggle to preserve his faith in the face of the suffering and waste which surrounds him. Is this what J. Michael Yates' poem is doing? Is there any reference in the poem to the person mentioned in the title? should there be? . . . .
Why are sections of the poem presented in italics?
The image of the locomotive, in Part II, and the idea that "we were all made of almost all water," in Part V, have been used in other poems in this book. Does the fact that they have been used by other poets weaken the image and the idea in this poem?

MARIA

Within her purple goblet,
Maria swims.
Outside the world condenses.

She doesn't miss anything anymore.
Events turn on the crystal curve
Or escape altogether her senses.

Things are too much without us,
I said,
Just over the sill of sense.

She went.
My words went after her.
Darkly. In waves. Like a plague of insects.

Half the next afternoon
I watched a poisoned ant
Reel along a table-edge.

Dreadful to see time passing in the distance.
Worse: to see nothing,
Hear its whistle. Only.

A tear slid
Between her eye
And sight.

I thought all along
She was one of those women who pass through a cloud
Through your life a bird through space.

Memory, my old egg,
Broke upon my head,
Dripped into my eyes.

My mind's reach groped for her
A hand in the dark
For a key before a door.

Unable not to stand her any longer
I came with the murderous vengeance of a child
And a madman's innocence.

When I race my wet finger
Around her goblet-lip,
She—or the glass itself—sings like a violin.

What is the purple goblet within which Maria swims?
What is the meaning of the third stanza? Is there an allusion here to Wordsworth's sonnet "The World is too Much with us"?

Again and again I go away from you and send back only words. Where I am is very cold and the ice figures I collect for you never, somehow, survive the transport. And so these small black tracks upon the page. Where you are is too warm for me. This message is a map which shows my exact coordinates at this moment. Follow it. Try to find me. I should like to be here when you arrive, but in this weather it is necessary to keep moving.

Is the "moving" a physical action, or is it something more?

J. Michael Yates

I persist in a little fabric between me and the world. This is the sleep inside a tent on an airless, sunstung afternoon. The sleep beyond mosquitoes and black flies that close in and in upon the beast that ceases to stir. This is the orange sleep that seeps and clings like mire. The muskeg and the clear streams are going away. the wet sleep comes for me like water on the rise. Snow-caps in the distance are burning. Somewhere in the extinguishing light, the plume of a crowning forest fire. Whatever will enter this canvas crypt can have me. Nothing comes, and I can't rise. The tick of a clock somewhere beneath things diminishes with the last fly that circles outside like a plane coming to rescue the lost in sleep. The mouth of flat blackness is closing. Sleep stiffens through me to the bayous beyond dream. I shall die here in this uncertain growth. Seams of the tent will give, canvas and skin will sink beneath the ash of the fire that has been burning toward me forever. The wind changes. The fire goes green. This is the sleep of mastodons and mammoths; this is not the sleep of winter bears I've buried beneath cornices of words. On the surface of the tar-pit, stillness over the blackness signals the stop of a monstrous metabolism. The undergrowth is zombied in the thin stutter of heat. The coming destruction. The roads I followed here are washing away. This is the Lazarus who returned with no more to show than a yawn, the taste of dying in his mouth, vague hunger, thirst and no recollection of awakening at an earlier dawn. This was the sleep within the tent that I sewed. I entered, shut out the weather and went to sleep for darkness' sake. The afternoon and the insects have waited. I dream I only dream I am awake.

Pretend you are observing the actions of the poet when he has the experience recounted above. What does he seem to be doing? What is he actually experiencing?
What is the relevance of the reference to Lazarus? (You might consult the Bible for stories on two men named Lazarus: see John 11 and Luke 16.)

In the blood-coloured cage
Behind my ribs
The lion circles.

In his chest
Turns a silhouette of slow rage
Like a man with a lion in his chest.

CANTICLE FOR ELECTRONIC MUSIC No. 4

That I conceive myself a failure at last
Is probably one more dismal success:
I drift out of hope horizontally, feet first.

The clocks of all previous harmonize in an empty room.
All those earlier candles will burn hereafter.
The populace of my recollection persist in the ages they were.

I am closer to death than all the old people.
I shall have been closer after they die.
Trout in the high lakes follow a stricken fish.

I dwell now in this wilderness of fewer
And fewer words. Time, the bat, hangs
Upside-down in the darkness inside me.

All the now and future Aprils she will say:
Time to time you need a fresh misrepresentation
Of yourself. There is probably nothing to say.

Ancient words which mean in deep roots
Of trees long since fallen: silence
Returns to silence through sound.

I desire, sometimes, a woman between me
And the sharp stone geography of light:
In first colour, objects collide into my eyes.

Think nothing in a land not land and not water.
In your vocabulary of flowers and fishes, say I was
A man stumbling through a crowd shouting his own name.

A canticle is a song or hymn of praise. Yet the poet sings only of a "dismal success." What is the poet praising—the moment when "silence / Returns to silence through sound"? Why, at the end of the poem, does the poet see himself as "man stumbling through a crowd shouting his own name"?

OTHER PUBLICATIONS

1. *Magazines that publish Canadian poetry*
    The Canadian Forum, 56 Esplanade St. E., Toronto 1, Ont.
    The Fiddlehead, University of New Brunswick, Fredericton, N.B.
    New: American and Canadian Poetry, R.D. 3, Trumansburg, New York, U.S.A.
    Prism International, Department of Creative Writing, University of British Columbia, Vancouver, B.C.
    Quarry, Box 1061, Kingston, Ont.
    The Tamarack Review, Box 159, Postal Station K, Toronto 12, Ont.
    West Coast Review, Simon Fraser University, Burnaby 413, B.C.
2. *Writer's guide (complete market list)*
    Eileen Goodman, *The Canadian Writer's Market,* McClelland & Stewart, 1970
3. *Principle anthologies*
    Ralph Gustafson, editor, *The Penguin Book of Canadian Verse,* 1967
    A. J. M. Smith, editor, *The Oxford Book of Canadian Verse,* 1960
    A. J. M. Smith, editor, *Modern Canadian Verse,* 1967
4. *Active anthologies*
    Peter Anson, editor, *Canada First,* House of Anansi, 1969
    Jim Brown and David Phillips, editors, *West Coast Seen,* Talon Books, 1969
    John Robert Colombo, editor, *How Do I Love Thee,* M. G. Hurtig, 1970
    Doug Fetherling, editor, *Thumbprints,* Peter Martin Associates, 1969
    John Glassco, editor, *The Poetry of French Canada in Translation,* Oxford University Press, 1970
    Dennis Lee, editor, *T. O. Now,* House of Anansi, 1969
    Douglas Lochhead and Raymond Souster, editors, *Made in Canada,* Oberon Press, 1970
    Jack Ludwig and Andy Wainwright, editors, *Soundings,* House of Anansi, 1970
    Eli Mandel and Jean-Guy Pilon, editors, *Poetry 62/Poésie 62,* The Ryerson Press, 1961
    Alfred Purdy, editor, *Storm Warning,* McClelland & Stewart, 1971
    Raymond Souster, editor, *New Wave Canada,* Contact Press, 1966
    J. Michael Yates, editor, *Contemporary Poetry of British Columbia,* Sono Nis, 1970